CANON LAW AND REALISM
Monsignor W. Onclin Chair 2000

KATHOLIEKE UNIVERSITEIT LEUVEN
Faculteit Kerkelijk Recht
Faculty of Canon Law

CANON LAW AND REALISM

Monsignor W. Onclin Chair 2000

UITGEVERIJ PEETERS
LEUVEN
2000

C.I.P. Koninklijke Bibliotheek Albert I

ISBN 90-429-0879-3
D.2000/0602/84

© 2000 Uitgeverij Peeters, Bondgenotenlaan 153, B-3000 Leuven (Belgium)

INHOUDSTAFEL / TABLE OF CONTENTS

DE ADVOCAAT IN DE KERK,
OF DE AVONTUREN VAN EEN VREEMDELING
IN HET PARADIJS

RIK TORFS

VOORGESCHIEDENIS: DE ADVOCAAT TUSSEN CONCILIE EN CODEX

Hoe de kerk precies moet worden gedefinieerd, is vakwerk voor bedreven theologen. Dat ze onder meer beoogt een geloofsgemeenschap te zijn en dat deze laatste notie in principe een positieve bijklank heeft, zullen inmiddels echter maar weinigen ontkennen. Er heerst in de kerk dus een positieve sfeer, theologisch kan dat niet anders. Conflicten, en ook advocaten die daar steevast mee worden geassocieerd, lijken daarbij niet meteen op hun plaats. Die spanning werd altijd al scherp aangevoeld, waardoor de rol van de advocaat in het kerkelijk recht als het ware structureel ter discussie stond.

Natuurlijk, rozige plaatjes wekken argwaan. Perfectie is onmogelijk. De Frans-Roemeense auteur E. M. Cioran wees daar overtuigend op: "Le paradis n'était pas supportable, sinon le premier homme s'en serait accommodé.[1]" Toch is het de spanning tussen de kerk als harmonische geloofsgemeenschap enerzijds, en de met conflicten geassocieerde positie van de advocaat anderzijds, die in de periode tussen Vaticanum II en de promulgatie van de nieuwe Codex (1965-1983) een enthousiaste houding ten aanzien van de advocaat in het canonieke recht in de weg hebben gestaan.

Wie in die tijd aan kerkelijke advocaten beschouwingen wijdde, had meteen het huwelijksrecht in zijn achterhoofd. Het was immers het terrein *par excellence* waarop het procesrecht zich manifesteerde. Dat gegeven leverde trouwens twee bijkomende redenen op om zich voor het inschakelen van een advocaat en voor diens mogelijke capriolen extra te hoeden.

---

[1] Het citaat komt uit *De l'inconvénient d'être né*, gepubliceerd in Parijs in 1973 bij Gallimard. Het werd opgenomen in zijn verzameld werk, E. M. CIORAN, *Œuvres*, Parijs, Gallimard Duarto, 1999, 1278.

Vooreerst streeft het huwelijksproces, minstens in theorie, niets anders na dan het achterhalen van de waarheid[2]. En zo is er maar één. Terwijl in een profane echtscheidingsprocedure partijen niet zelden de messen scherpen om gelijk te *halen,* zijn ze in een canoniek proces op zoek naar de *waarheid.* Mogelijk hebben beide partijen zelfs exact hetzelfde standpunt, en delen ze de overtuiging dat het huwelijk nietig is, bijvoorbeeld wegens *metus reverentialis,* door eerbied geïnspireerde vrees, in hoofde van de vrouw. Het huwelijksproces heeft immers een declaratoir, en geen contradictoir karakter[3]. Echte belangentegenstellingen tussen de partijen zijn er niet, weshalve een advocaat in wezen overbodig is: ongeveer zo klinkt een vooral bij theologen vaak gehoorde argumentatie. Natuurlijk overtuigt zo'n redenering niet echt: ook al staat de waarheid centraal, de wijze waarop ze wordt gevonden, met alle kwetsuren die zulk een zoektocht kan opleveren, rechtvaardigt op zichzelf al de aanwezigheid van een advocaat[4]. Sommige gelovigen verkiezen bovendien een boude *non constat de nullitate* boven de triomf van een vernederende waarheid waarin ze zichzelf niet herkennen. En of er bij een huwelijksprocedure *echt* geen tegengestelde belangen zijn, komt verder nog aan bod. Maar goed, de rol van de advocaat zal in het raam van het canonieke huwelijksrecht minstens anders ogen dan in een louter seculiere context, wat de scepsis die in het verleden zo kenmerkend was voor de rol van de advocaat alvast enigszins begrijpelijk maakt.

Het tweede argument tegen de advocaat reikt nog een stapje verder. Het luidt als volgt: niet alleen gaat het bij een canonieke nietigheidsprocedure allerminst om een gewoon contentieus geschil, eigenlijk is de hele zaak niet eens een juridische kwestie. De aanpak van het tribunaal moet wezenlijk pastoraal zijn[5]. Rechters en auditeurs, vaak priesters met

[2] Cf. IOANNES PAULUS PP. II, *Ad Tribunalis Sacrae Romanae Rotae Decanum, Praelatos Auditores, Officiales et Advocatos, novo Litibus iudicandis ineunte anno: de veritate iustititiae matre,* 4.2.1980, *AAS,* 1980, 172-178, 174: "Tutti gli atti del giudizio ecclesiastico, dal libello alle scritture di difesa, possono e debbono essere fonte di verità (...)." Cf. ook K. HARTELT, "Liebe und Recht. Anmerkungen zur theologischen Grundlegung des Kirchenrechts", in K. LÜDICKE, H. PAARHAMMER en D.A. BINDER (ed.), *Recht im Dienste des Menschen. Eine Festgabe Hugo Schwendenwein zum 60. Geburtstag,* Graz, Styria, 1986, 328.
[3] A. JACOBS, *Le droit de la défense dans les procès en nullité de mariage,* Parijs, Éditions du Cerf, 1998, 438; 509.
[4] R. TORFS, "Le droit de la défense dans les procès en nullité de mariage. Quelques réflexions à propos d'un livre d'Ann Jacobs", *Revue de droit canonique,* 1998, 45 e.s.
[5] Cf. P.J.M. HUIZING, "Schets voor herzien canoniek huwelijksrecht", in J.H.A. VAN TILBORG, TH.A.G. VAN EUPEN en P.J.M. HUIZING, *Alternatief kerkelijk huwelijksrecht,* Bilthoven, Amboboeken, 1974, 37-53. Op p. 37 gaat Huizing als volgt van start: "De volgende schets bedoelt niet een volledig ontwerp te zijn voor een nieuw in te voeren

ruime ervaring in het veld, zijn perfect uitgerust om er pastoraal stevig tegenaan te gaan zonder dat derden, advocaten bijvoorbeeld, koele bedienaars van de wet, daarbij betrokken hoeven te worden. Integendeel: hun lastige vragen nemen het *momentum* weg. Wat bepaalde kerkelijke rechtbanken in de jaren zeventig en tachtig boden, was een louter pastorale benadering die post factum, louter en alleen *pour les besoins de la cause*, in een procedureel keurslijf werd gestopt[6]. De door betrokkenen als pastorale gesprekken aangevoelde contacten werden *achteraf* gedefinieerd als, bijvoorbeeld, de ondervraging van een partij door de rechter. Een Nederlands pastor toonde en toont zich zelfs een voorstander van scheidingsvieringen, waarbij best wel een potje mag worden gejankt[7], onder de goedmoedige begeleiding van een pastor. Dergelijke aanpak was en is onverenigbaar met het kerkelijk huwelijksrecht. Hij verliest ook veld. Privacy is vandaag belangrijk[8], en de idee dat volledige openheid over het algehele leven nodig is om elk huwelijksmysterie finaal te ontsluieren, is op haar retour. Nu. Maar in de periode tussen 1965 en 1983, toen binnenkerkelijk in feite sprake was van een vorm van juridisch vacuüm, werd de schijnbare onverenigbaarheid tussen een "pastorale" procedure en de inbreng van de advocaat geregeld in alle scherpte aangevoeld.

Ondanks de twee zopas beschreven argumenten tegen elke rol van de advocaat in het kerkelijk recht, meer bepaald in het huwelijksrecht, verkreeg hij toch een plaats in het kerkelijk wetboek van 1983. De klemtoon ligt in de Codex nog steeds bij advocatenwerk in het raam van het huwelijksrecht[9]. Maar van de advocaat wordt onder

canoniek huwelijksrecht, maar slechts een eerste schematische aanzet voor een gedachtenwisseling over de richting waarin een pastoraal georiënteerde kerkelijke huwelijksorde zich zou kunnen ontwikkelen."

[6] Soms geschiedde zulks op een briljante manier. Cf. O.F. TER REEGEN, "La jurisprudence hollandaise", *Revue de droit canonique*, 1990, 167-178.

[7] Zie hiervoor L. GOERTZ, "Kerkelijke rechtbanken aan het einde van hun Latijn? Scheiden zonder juridisch gesol", *de Bazuin*, 5 september 1997, 4-6. Het potje janken prijkt op p. 5. Op dezelfde pagina schrijft Goertz: "In juridische zin lijkt me een kerkelijke rechtbank (...) overbodig. Wel zie ik daarvoor een andere, nieuwe taak: als pastoraal adviesbureau optreden voor individuen, echtparen en pastores die bij de ingrijpende kwesties van de menselijke relaties op hoger niveau graag verder geholpen willen worden."

[8] Ook in het kerkelijk wetboek wordt de privacy beschermd, namelijk in canon 220. Zie hierover bijvoorbeeld A. CAUTERUCCIO, "Il diritto alla buona fama ed alla intimità. Analisi e commento del can. 220", *Commentarium pro religiosis*, 1992, 39-81.

[9] Bij de *ratum sed non consummatum*-procedure is de advocaat evenwel verboden, cf. canon 1701 §2. Zie hierover H. PREE, "Die Rechtsstellung des advocatus und des procurator im kanonischen Prozeßrecht", in W. AYMANS en K.-TH. GERINGER (ed.), *Iuri Canonici Promovendo. Festschrift für Heribert Schmitz zum 65. Geburtstag*, Regensburg, Friedrich Pustet, 1994, 315-318.

meer[10] ook melding gemaakt in het mondeling contentieus proces (can. 1663-1664), het strafproces (can. 1723 en 1725) en, wellicht erg belangrijk in de toekomst, het hiërarchisch beroep (can. 1738). Het gegeven dat de advocaat nu eenmaal in het wetboek zijn opwachting maakt, en zulks op diverse plaatsen, zorgt meteen voor een nieuw discussieveld. De vraag luidt niet langer: is de advocaat op zijn plaats in de kerk? Voortaan presenteert ze zich anders: *hoe* past de advocaat in het rechtssysteem van de kerk? Hoe integreert hij zich in een subcultuur die niet meteen de zijne is? Daarna komt een vraag die nog een stuk lastiger is: op welke wijze treedt de advocaat in interactie met zwaar theologisch gekleurde rechtsfiguren, zoals bijvoorbeeld het incardinatiebeginsel? Recht op verdediging en incardinatie... De begrippen vloeken een beetje, zoals gulzigheid niet past bij een mysticus of ironie haaks staat op het ernstige beroep van kerkjurist.

DE ADVOCAAT IN HET RECHTSSYSTEEM VAN DE KERK

De advocaat wordt erkend door het kerkelijk recht. Zijn profiel wordt in canon 1483 geschetst. Hij moet meerderjarig[11] zijn en van goede naam. Volgens een verklaring van de Apostolische Signatuur van 12 juli 1993 ontbreekt die goede naam bij een advocaat die in een zogenaamde *onregelmatige relatie* leeft[12]. Verder hoort hij katholiek[13] te zijn, tenzij de diocesane bisschop het anders toestaat. Hij dient over een doctoraat in het canoniek recht te beschikken of anderszins werkelijk deskundig te zijn. Tenslotte moet hij door de bisschop

[10] Voor meer details over speciale categorieën van advocaten en dossiers, zie C.P. PEÑARROYA, *Abogados y procuradores en la Curia Romana*, Rome, E.V., 1996, 432 p.

[11] Meerderjarigheid betekent dat hij het achttiende levensjaar heeft voltooid. Zie canon 97 §1.

[12] Cf. "Acta Tribunalium S. Sedis. Supremum Signaturae Apostolicae Tribunal. Prot. N 24339/93 V.T.", *Periodica*, 1993, 699-700. In zijn commentaar ziet Raymond Burke de gevolgen van die onregelmatige relatie ruim: "... qui vivit in unione irregulari ad exercendum munus advocati admitti nequit. Hoc principium, quatenus generale, per se valet pro advocato ad casum admittendo, pro advocato in albo advocatorum inscribendo, et pro advocato iam in albo inscripto." Het recht op *privacy* delft dus het onderspit.

[13] Klaus Lüdicke meent dat het passend is (*angemessen*) dat de advocaat de kerk niet heeft verlaten bij formele akt. Zie K. LÜDICKE, "Prozeßrecht: Parteien", in K. LÜDICKE, (ed.), *Münsterischer Kommentar zum Codex Iuris Canonici*, V, Essen, Ludgerus, losbladig, 1483/2. Strikt genomen is dit geen vereiste. Maar in samenhang met de verplichte eed (can. 1454) en de ruime bevoegdheid waarover de diocesane bisschop bij de goedkeuring van de advocaat beschikt, heeft Lüdicke het voor wat de praktijk betreft wellicht bij het rechte eind.

worden goedgekeurd[14]. Uit dit lijstje blijkt dat de bisschop over een ruime marge beschikt om de advocaat niet te aanvaarden. Zelfs als laatstgenoemde een katholiek doctor in het kerkelijk recht is, kan hij de woestijn worden ingestuurd omdat hij naar het oordeel van de bisschop niet over een goede naam beschikt. Bovendien kan diezelfde bisschop hem ook zonder nadere motivering een goedkeuring weigeren[15]. Indien zulks op stilzwijgende manier gebeurt, is hiertegen zelfs geen hiërarchisch beroep mogelijk. Eens aanvaard, moet de advocaat bovendien een eed afleggen[16].

De wezenlijke moeilijkheid in verband met de positie van de advocaat ligt echter niet hier. De persoon van de advocaat telt uiteraard mee, maar hoe hij kan werken is een stuk wezenlijker. Doorslaggevend is derhalve de meer theoretische vraag, maar dan een vraag met erg praktische consequenties, welke rol een advocaat *werkelijk* te spelen heeft in een systeem dat de scheiding – of noem het met een modernere term *evenwicht*[17] – van machten niet aanvaardt. In Westerse democratieën zijn wij een dergelijke vraagstelling niet gewoon. Duidelijk is alvast dat de rol van de advocaat varieert naarmate de concrete binnenkerkelijke situatie waarin hij optreedt, verschilt. Op een aantal terreinen zal de rol van de advocaat niet echt anders zijn dan die welke zijn profaanrechtelijke collega zoal vermag te vervullen; op andere gebieden is het verschil evenwel op ieder moment tastbaar aanwezig[18]. Ten aanzien van de rol van de canonieke advocaat dient zich een onderscheid aan tussen drie verschillende terreinen:

[14] Dit gebeurt door een decreet. Cf. verder H. PREE, "Die Rechtsstellung ...", in W. AYMANS e.a. (ed.), *o.c.*, 305: "Die Approbation gilt nur für das Gericht des approbierenden Bischofs. Einer zusätzlichen Bestellung durch den Vorsitzenden des kirchlichen Gerichtshofes bedarf es nicht."

[15] J. Weier vraagt precisere normen met betrekking tot de goedkeuring door de bisschop: J. WEIER, "Der Anwalt im kirchlichen Eheprozess. Neue Bestimmungen im CIC", in A. GABRIELS en H. J. F. REINHARDT (ed.), *Ministerium Iustitiae. Festschrift für Heribert Heinemann*, Essen, Ludgerus, 1985, 408. Ten aanzien van de deelname van advocaten aan verhoren worden strictere normen voor het weren van een advocaat gevraagd door diezelfde J. WEIER, "Die Parität zwischen Ehebandverteidiger und Anwalt im kirchlichen Ehenichtigkeitsprozeß - Erreichtes und Erwünschtes", *De processibus matrimonialibus*, 1997, 333.

[16] Zie canon 1454. Cf. hierover ook H. PREE, "Die Rechtsstellung ...", in W. AYMANS e.a. (ed.), *o.c.*, 305.

[17] Cf. W.J. WITTEVEEN, *Evenwicht van machten*, Zwolle, Tjeenk Willink, 1991, 100 p.

[18] H. PREE, "Die Rechtsstellung ...", in W. AYMANS e.a. (ed.), *o.c.*, 313-314 onderscheidt drie doelstellingen van de rechtsbijstand, namelijk (1) deskundige bijstand in de procesdialectiek; (2) streven naar convergentie tussen formele en materiële waarheid; (3) de proceseconomie, dus de verwachting dat het geding *citius, melius ac minoribus sumptibus* verloopt.

(1) Het gewone *contentieuze proces* tussen twee partijen verschilt in de kerk weinig van de profaanrechtelijke discussie. Het gaat immers om een conflict waarvan de theologische relevantie eerder marginaal is of geheel afwezig blijft. Bovendien is de kerkelijke overheid bij het geding geen betrokken partij. Die twee factoren maken dat de geladenheid van het dossier beperkt blijft. Enkele voorbeelden ter verduidelijking. Een discussie over een legaat, over een beneficie, over bepaalde gevolgen van een contract, uiteraard in de hypothese dat dergelijke dossiers aan een kerkelijke rechtbank worden voorgelegd, wat niet al te vaak het geval is wegens het directer nut dat veelal met een louter profane procedure gepaard gaat, hebben twee dingen gemeen: theologisch staat er niet veel op het spel en de kerkelijke overheid is geen betrokken partij. Het gevolg hiervan is helder: in zulk een contentieus proces beschikt de advocaat over mogelijkheden die nauw aanleunen bij wat een profaan advocaat zoal vermag in een gelijkaardige situatie.

(2) Het *huwelijksproces* bekleedt een middenpositie. Aan de ene kant wordt het gekenmerkt door de theologische specificiteit van het canonieke huwelijksrecht. Boven werd daar reeds gewag van gemaakt; men denke aan het declaratoire karakter van de procedure. De procedure moet zich immers noodgedwongen tot een onderzoek naar de geldigheid van het huwelijk beperken, omdat de ontbinding op theologische gronden wordt afgewezen. De advocaat dient zich op dit terrein dus aan te passen en speelt een rol die hij op het profane terrein niet krijgt aangeboden. Het touwtrekken met het oog op een gunstige echtscheidingsregeling maakt plaats voor een scrupuleuze zoektocht naar een ontologische waarheid, zo al niet in de praktijk dan toch minstens vanuit rechtstheoretisch oogpunt. Hoe aardig kan de advocaat, die aan zulk een proces van waarheidsvinding deelachtig wordt, zich opstellen tegenover zijn cliënt? Waar ligt zijn uiteindelijke loyaliteit? Allicht niet exact dàr, waar ze bij de profane advocaat zou te situeren zijn. Sommige advocaten leven zich in hun specifieke kerkelijke rol bijzonder sterk in en schrijven een pleidooi waarin ze, in naam van de waarheid, hun cliënt zonder diens medeweten onderuit halen[19]. Vooral

---

[19] Dat de advocaat toch wel echt ten voordele van zijn cliënt mag argumenteren, blijkt uit de in noot 2 vermelde allocutio van paus Johannes-Paulus II. In *AAS*, 1980, 175 leest men: "Ad aiutare quest'opera delicata ed importante dei giudici sono ordinate le 'defensiones' degli Avvocati, le 'animadversiones' del Difensore del Vinculo, l'eventuale voto del Promotore di Giustizia. Anche costoro nello svolgere il loro compito, i primi in favore delle parti, il secondo in difesa del vinculo, il terzo in 'iure inquirendo', devono servire alla verità, perché trionfi la giustizia." Een gelijkaardige openheid wordt ook vertoond in *Communicationes*, 1984, 64 e.v.

bij een advocaat die zich erg pastoraal opstelt en die aan de waarheidsvinding een voor zijn cliënt helende functie verbindt, bestaat dit
risico. Anderen zullen dan weer het principe van de waarheidsvinding accepteren, zonder zichzelf daarbij een hoofdrol toe te bedelen:
de waarheid zoeken is heel aardig, maar ook dan heeft een partij verdediging nodig[20]. Uiteindelijk is het aan de rechtbank om haar verantwoordelijkheid te nemen. Kortom: de theologische specificiteit
van de huwelijksprocedure dwingt de advocaat zijn strategie, en mis-
schien zelfs zijn geestesgesteltenis, aan te passen[21]. Aan de andere
kant is het evenwel zo dat, bij het huwelijksproces, de overheid niet
onmiddellijk betrokken partij is. Deze gedachte verdient uiteraard
enige nuancering. Zenon Grocholewski ziet in de procedure tot nie-
tigverklaring een waarachtig rechtsgeding waarbij de partner die de
nietigheid aanvoert de eiser is en de kerk zelf, vertegenwoordigd
door de *defensor vinculi,* als tegenpartij fungeert. De *conventus*
wordt door Grocholewski als een tussenkomende derde in de zin van
canon 1596 beschouwd[22]. Niet iedereen gaat hiermee akkoord.
Lüdicke ziet het huwelijksproces naar mijn aanvoelen terecht als
een gerechtelijke vaststelling van een *factum iuridicum*[23]. Maar zelfs
als men de opvatting van Grocholewski op een theoretisch niveau
aanvaardt, impliceert ze nog geen praktische betrokkenheid van de

[20] In een aantal landen treedt de advocaat pas in beroep aan, zie hierover bv. L.
ZIMMERMANN, "Die Mitwirkung des Anwalts im kanonischen Eheprozeß. Praktische
Erfahrungen und Anregungen", in R. PUZA en A. WEISS (ed.), *Iustitia in caritate. Festgabe für Ernst Rößler zum 25jährigen Dienstjubiläum als Offizial der Diözese Rottenburg-Stuttgart,* Frankfurt am Main/Berlijn/Bern/New York/Parijs/Wenen, Peter Lang,
1997, 447. Het is duidelijk dat in die hypothese gedegen rechtsbijstand belangrijker is dan
pastorale hulp. Indien deze laatste centraal had gestaan, zou de advocaat wellicht reeds
naar aanleiding van de procedure in eerste aanleg gecontacteerd zijn geweest.
[21] Cf. S. GHERRO, "Il diritto alla difesa nell'ordinamento canonico", *Monitor Ecclesiasticus,* 1988, 2, wijst heel sterk op de specificiteit van het huwelijksrecht. De verbinding van het *giusto* en het *vero* is geen sinecure: "L'affermazione trova peculiare riscontro quanto alle cause matrimoniali, giacché, tramite le medesime, si persegue
esclusivamente *l'accertamento* di un *quid* che rileva nell'ordine giuridico degli uomini,
ma che implica contemporanea incidenza in quello soprannaturale dei rapporti con la
Divinità."
[22] Z. GROCHOLEWSKI, "Quisnam est pars conventa in causis nullitatis matrimonii?",
Periodica, 1990, 357-391.
[23] K. LÜDICKE, "Der kirchliche Ehenichtichkeitsprozeß. Ein processus contentiosus?", *Österreichisches Archiv für Kirchenrecht,* 1990, 299. Tegen de stelling van
Grocholewski argumenteert ook R. AHLERS, "Der Stellenwert des Verteidigungsrechtes
im Ehenichtigkeitsverfahren", *De processibus matrimonialibus,* 1995, 289. Ten aanzien
van de verdediger van de huwelijksband stelt zij: "Er schützt das öffentliche Interesse der
Kirche und tritt für die Gültigkeit der Ehe ein, er personifiziert diese aber nicht."

kerkelijke overheid. Zeker, het huwelijk heeft niet alleen privaat[24], maar ook publiek belang[25]; doch de overheid als overheid voelt zich door het geding niet direct aangesproken. Dit werkt dedramatiserend en verklaart ook waarom, naar aanleiding van huwelijksdossiers, de kerkelijke overheid zich zelden bijzonder opwindt.

(3) Het *strafproces* en het *hiërarchisch beroep annex het mogelijke vatten van een administratieve rechtbank*[26] gaan een stap verder. De overheid is nu wel bij het geding betrokken. Als rechter, als administrator, als partij. Bovendien geschiedt dit, zoals al aangegeven, in een wat onzeker makende context waarbij de scheiding of het evenwicht van machten niet bestaat, een gegeven dat zelf gebaseerd is op theologische vooronderstellingen, zoals de theologische positie van de bisschoppen als opvolgers van de apostelen en van de paus als opvolger van Petrus. Maar ook al kan de bestaande context helder worden verklaard, ook al is hij theologisch mogelijk onafwendbaar, dan nog wordt de situatie er niet minder hachelijk door. Hoe kan een advocaat zijn draai vinden in procedures, zoals het hiërarchische beroep, waarin een bisschop die in een conflict is gewikkeld met zijn priester, tegelijk rechter en partij is, althans wanneer men de bestaande canonieke situatie vertaalt naar de profaanrechtelijke perceptie ervan? Een concreet voorbeeld: als een advocaat, in het raam van canon 1734, aan een bisschop vraagt om zijn eigen decreet te herroepen of te verbeteren, is het wellicht niet aangewezen daarbij de klemtoon te leggen op gemaakte juridische fouten. De bisschop vindt een dergelijke argumentatie wellicht niet écht leuk. Meestal zal de advocaat zich pragmatisch uit de slag pogen te trekken, en dit in het volle bewustzijn van zijn inferieure positie. Immers, in een configuratie waarbij iemand geroepen wordt om zijn eigen administratieve beslissing te beoordelen, is het wellicht aangewezen een eerder juridisch pleidooi in te ruilen voor een doordacht en uitgebalanceerd smeekschrift. De verstrengeling van administratieve macht en beoordelende instantie maakt dat een zakelijk-juridische benadering het risico loopt contraproductief uit te pakken.

---

[24] In een decreet coram Agustoni van 17 maart 1976 leest men dat in dossiers waarin zowel van privaat als van publiek belang sprake is, zoals het huwelijksproces, de advocaat zich beperkt tot de verdediging van de private belangen van partijen. Zie hierover G. ERLEBACH, *La nullità della sentenza giudiziale 'ob ius defensionis denegatum' nella giurisprudenza rotale,* Vaticaanstad, Libreria Editrice Vaticana, 1991, 230.

[25] R. AHLERS, *o.c.,* 289.

[26] Rechtsbijstand is mogelijk als *pars resistens* en als *pars recurrens.* Cf. Z. GROCHOLEWSKI, "L'autorità amministrativa come ricorrente alla Sectio Altera della Segnatura Apostolica", *Apollinaris,* 1982, 770-779.

Tot zover de drie categorieën. De indeling van het werkveld van de canonieke advocaat in drie verschillende subterreinen kan grafisch worden voorgesteld in drie cirkels.

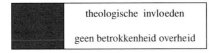

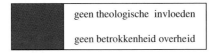

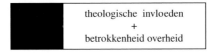

De *buitencirkel* toont de procedures van de eerste categorie. De problematiek is nauwelijks of niet theologisch gekleurd en de overheid is geen betrokken partij.

De *middencirkel* omvat procedures die wel theologisch zijn ingekleurd, maar de overheid is nog steeds niet in haar hoedanigheid van overheid bij het geding betrokken. De advocaat moet zich mentaal aanpassen, maar heeft procedureel nog heel wat speelruimte.

De *binnencirkel* combineert theologische geladenheid met een min of meer directe betrokkenheid van de overheid. De advocaat bevindt zich in een erg onzekere positie en valt geregeld terug op semi-juridische onderhandelingsstrategieën.

Naarmate de kern van de grafische voorstelling dichterbij komt, neemt de rol van de advocaat een meer atypische vorm aan. Hoe kan hij tot in de binnencirkel toe, in een systeem zonder evenwicht van machten, zo onafhankelijk mogelijk zijn rol blijven vervullen? Het kerkelijk wetboek gaat op deze vraag niet echt in, wat mij een positief gegeven lijkt. Teveel tekst zou mogelijke contradicties blootleggen, zonder ze te kunnen oplossen. Ook de particuliere wetgever zou best terughoudend blijven, zeker wanneer zijn wetgeving ertoe zou strekken, onder het mom van stroomlijning, de functioneringsmogelijkheden en de actieradius van de advocaat in te perken[27]. Wanneer de advocaat, die structureel reeds vanuit een zwakke positie moet opereren[28], ook nog eens met een strak diocesaan statuut wordt geconfronteerd, dreigt zijn positie wel erg wankel te worden. De wetgever die hem de normen van een strak statuut oplegt, is immers dezelfde als de administrator die een decreet uitvaardigde, dezelfde ook als de instantie die dit decreet weer kan herroepen of verbeteren. Een diocesaan statuut maakt de symbiose van de machten er alleen maar completer op. Theologisch piekfijn in orde natuurlijk, maar toch ook juridisch beklemmend.

Maar terug naar de grafische voorstelling en haar consequenties: naarmate de binnencirkel dichterbij komt, wordt de juridische garantie van een inhoudelijk en kwalitatief volwaardig recht op verdediging

---

[27] Ook bijkomende vereisten voor benoeming, naast die van het universele recht, kunnen belemmerend werken. Cf. F.J. RAMOS, "Considerazioni sulla necessità dell'intervento degli avvocati nei processi di dichiarazione di nullità del matrimonio canonico", *Ius Ecclesiae*, 1998, 290.

[28] Hij staat bijvoorbeeld nog steeds niet op het niveau van de verdediger van de huwelijksband.

problematischer. Tegelijk wordt de taak van de advocaat moeilijker. De discussie draait immers al heel gauw om de waarheid, en de beoordelende instanties verkeren niet in een positie waarin ze gemakkelijk wat afstand kunnen nemen. Op het niveau van het *harde recht*, het niveau van wettelijke garanties valt aan dit euvel niet te verhelpen. Theologische vereisten, zeker wanneer ze zijn gebaseerd op goddelijk recht, primeren op louter juridische normen die een behoorlijke rechtsbedeling garanderen of het recht op verdediging gestalte trachten te geven. Wie canoniek recht beoefent, moet zich daar *rebus sic stantibus* bij neerleggen, wat hij er diep in zijn hart ook moge over denken. Maar al zijn wettelijke garanties in de lijn van de democratische rechtsstaat ten enen male onmogelijk, er kunnen toch *niet-bindende richtlijnen* worden ontwikkeld, die de kerkelijke overheid in haar functie van *wetgever-administrator-beoordelende instantie* in alle vrijheid tot de hare kan maken. Ik leg er de nadruk op: in alle vrijheid. Er is geen enkele verplichting, tenzij men canon 221 en de *due process*-principes ook binnenkerkelijk als formeel superieure normen zou willen beschouwen, wat mij nog altijd de weg van de toekomst lijkt[29]. Tegelijk moet echter worden toegegeven dat het formele overwicht van de plichten en rechten van alle christengelovigen ten opzichte van andere rechtsnormen weliswaar bijval vindt bij een deel van de rechtsleer[30], maar zeker niet algemeen wordt aanvaard of toegepast door de practici van het canonieke recht. Doch ook zonder die wettelijk verankerde formele superioriteit zouden *niet-bindende richtlijnen* de geloofwaardigheid van het canonieke rechtsysteem een niet onaardig duwtje in de rug kunnen geven. Laten we het daar, althans in deze bijdrage, op houden.

In de titel die nu volgt, zou ik een richtlijn willen ontwikkelen voor de *hard core* van het systeem, voor casussen uit de absolute binnencirkel. Als voorbeeld neem ik heel concreet een geval waarbij theologische concepten en figuren volop spelen, en waarbij de kerkelijke overheid tot en met betrokken partij is. Een waar moeras voor de advocaat, zoveel is zeker.

---

[29] Elders werkte ik die gedachte verder uit, onder meer tijdens een lezing gehouden te Weingarten op 27 november 1997 met als titel *Die Menschenrechte, die Grundrechte der Christen und das Kirchenrecht*. De tekst is in druk. Ook in druk is de tekst van een seminarie gehouden te Minneapolis op 5 oktober 1999 met als titel *Rights in Canon Law: Real, Ideal or Fluff?*

[30] Zie R. PUZA, "Der Rechtsschutz im Kirchenrecht zwischen Hierarchie und Grundrechten", *Theologische Quartalschrift*, 1999, 179-194.

DE ADVOCAAT IN DE BINNENCIRKEL

Vaker dan in het verleden nemen conflicten tussen priesters en hun bis-schop een formeel-juridische vorm aan. De weg van het hiërarchische beroep wordt bewandeld. Niet zelden wordt die keuze gemaakt nadat andere vormen van dialoog tussen de betrokkenen op niets zijn uitge-draaid. De formalisering van het meningsverschil wordt in dat perspectief als een laatste uitweg aangevoeld. Verwonderlijk is deze evolutie naar meer juridisering toe helemaal niet. Al blijft de relatie tussen de priester en de bisschop op het incardinatiebeginsel steunen, deze binnenkerkelijke verhouding schermt de *dramatis personae* niet langer af van externe invloeden. Het interne socialiseringsproces waaraan priesters worden onderworpen, is minder alomvattend dan in het verleden. De persoon van de priester verdwijnt niet langer helemaal achter zijn wijding: hij is ook consument, staatsburger, in zekere zin voelt hij zich zelfs werknemer, ook al zou dit laatste vanuit een gezonde wijdingstheologie niet mogen. De gevolgen van dit alles spreken voor zichzelf: steeds meer conflicten wor-den geformaliseerd. Maar terug nu naar het specifieke moment van die formalisering. Het is geen gemakkelijk ogenblik. Er is dan al heel wat irri-tatie. De priester doet een beroep op een advocaat omdat de traditionele gesprekssituatie priester/bisschop niet tot de gewenste resultaten leidt.

De formeel-juridische situatie nestelt zich naast een andere, theolo-gisch rijk uitgebouwde, rechtsfiguur, te weten de incardinatie[31]. Canon 265 legt incardinatie op voor iedere clericus[32]. Die moet zijn ordinaris eerbied en gehoorzaamheid betonen (can. 273). Daartegenover staat dan weer dat de ordinaris, bijvoorbeeld de diocesane bisschop, moet zorgen

---

[31] Paus Johannes-Paulus II biedt meer preciseringen in de postsynodale exhortatie *Pastores dabo vobis* van 25 maart 1992. Zie IOANNES PAULUS PP. II, Adhortatio apost-olica postsynodalis ad Episcopos, Sacerdotes et Christifideles totius Catholicae Ecclesiae, de Sacerdotium formatione in aetatis nostrae rerum condicione *Pastores dabo vobis*, 25.3.1992, *AAS*, 1992, 657-804. In nr. 31, p. 707-709, wordt benadrukt dat de incardina-tie meer is dan alleen maar een rechtsband. Zij brengt ook geestelijke en pastorale gevol-gen voort.

[32] Zie hierover bv. J.I. DONLON, "Incardination and Excardination: The Rights and Obligations of the Cleric and of the Church- A Matter of Pastoral Justice", in Canon Law Society of America (ed.), *Proceedings of the fifty-third Annual Convention*, Washington, CLSA, 1992, 124-153. Op p. 131 schrijft Donlon: "This provision of the law, a near res-tatement of the 1917 Code, is in keeping with the oldest traditions of the church. Under-lying this norm are two reasons. First, no individual should be inducted into the clerical state unless there is a need in the community for his service. As John Lynch points out in the CLSA commentary, 'private devotion, honor, and convenience are not sufficient jus-tification for ordination.' Second, the institute of incardination expresses a concern for stability within the ranks of the clergy."

voor een *honesta sustentatio*, passend levensonderhoud[33], alsmede sociale bijstand, volgens het recht (can. 384).

De zopas geschetste situatie is dus complex. En de vraag waar het daarbij om gaat is wezenlijk deze: op welk been kan de advocaat dansen in een geformaliseerd conflict tussen twee mensen die via de band van incardinatie tot elkaar veroordeeld zijn, maar die er toch even niet uitkomen? Eigenlijk is de vraagstelling zo complex, omdat hier twee sterk verschillende principes met elkaar worden verbonden, zonder dat een gemeenschappelijke factor hen bij elkaar brengt. Aan de ene kant staan de procesvoering en het recht van verdediging, dus twee juridische aspecten; aan de andere kant is er het incardinatiebeginsel, een theologisch stevig gegronde rechtsfiguur, die gezien haar intrinsieke diepgang elk formeel juridisch conflict overbodig zou moeten maken. Maar daar zit precies het probleem: *zou moeten maken*. De theologisch gezien onwenselijke hypothese van een formeel juridisch conflict doet zich toch voor. Alleen al dat gegeven is voor de betrokken kerkleider vaak een bron van irritatie. Begrijpelijk, want hij proeft in de formele escalatie van het conflict een stukje eigen falen. De vraag is dan: hoe kunnen het incardinatiebeginsel en de eigen rol van de advocaat in het geformaliseerde conflict op acceptabele wijze met elkaar in verbinding worden gebracht? Drie modellen zijn mogelijk. Daar zij kwalitatief allerminst gelijkwaardig zijn, worden zij hier niet in een vorm van juxtapositie aangeboden. Er is integendeel sprake van een gradatie, die begint bij een eerste, kwalitatief zwak, model, en eindigt met een derde model waarin, ook binnen een context van incardinatie, het recht op verdediging en de rol van de advocaat volledig ernstig worden genomen.

Eerste model:

Het *eerste model* accepteert uitsluitend het incardinatiebeginsel als aanknopingspunt voor verdere actie. De bisschop neemt, geheel in de lijn van canon 384, de rechten van zijn priesters, die zijn medewerkers en raadgevers zijn, in bescherming. Een conflict tussen de partners in de incardinatieband valt natuurlijk niet geheel en al uit te sluiten, maar moet helemaal binnen de figuur van diezelfde incardinatie worden gesitueerd (fig.1). Hoe wordt zo een houding zichtbaar? De bisschop kan bijvoorbeeld aan een priester weigeren met hem in gesprek te gaan in aanwezigheid van een advocaat, omdat de aanwezigheid van deze laatste de zuiverheid van de

---

[33] H. SCHMITZ, "Die Sustentation der Kleriker", in H. PAARHAMMER (ed.), *Vermögensverwaltung in der Kirche. Administratorum bonorum. Oeconomus tamquam paterfamilias. Sebastian Ritter zum 70. Geburtstag*, Thaur/Tirol, Echter, 1988, 177-191.

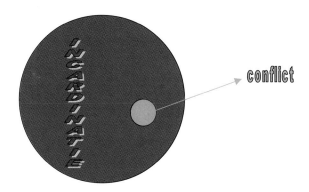

Figuur 1

incardinatieband zou verstoren[34]. Heinrich Flatten schreef ooit, met betrekking tot het huwelijksproces, dat de aanwezigheid van een advocaat bij het
verhoor van de partijen tot remmingen bij deze laatsten zou kunnen leiden.[35] Naar analogie hiermee zou kunnen worden betoogd dat de advocaat
voor gelijkaardige remmingen in het raam van de incardinatieverhouding
zorgt. Hij hindert de open dialoog tussen twee mensen die nauwer met
elkaar verbonden zijn dan alleen maar door een rechtsband: zo ongeveer
zou het bezwaar kunnen luiden. Canon 1738 stelt trouwens dat de indiener
van een beroep weliswaar het recht heeft om van een advocaat gebruik te
maken, maar vooraleer er formeel van een beroep sprake is, bestaat dit
recht nog niet. De bisschop heeft dus formeel het recht om elke interven-
tie van de advocaat te weigeren totdat het beroep wordt ingediend, een
regel die door Carlo Gullo terecht op de korrel werd genomen, maar die
nu eenmaal in het wetboek te lezen staat[36]. Niet zelden zal de bisschop dat
beroep trouwens associëren met een breuk van de vertrouwensband tussen
de priester en hemzelf. Kortom, in het aangehaalde voorbeeld bestaat
geen enkele constructieve dwarsverbinding tussen incardinatie en formeel
conflict. Het conflict moet binnen de vertrouwensband van de incardinatie worden uitgepraat. Zo eenvoudig liggen de zaken.

[34] Klaus Mörsdorf kwalificeerde de incardinatie als 'geistlichen Heimatverband'.
Deze terminologie heeft iets huiselijks. Zie hierover verder H.J.F. REINHARDT, "Volk
Gottes: die Kleriker", in K. LÜDICKE (ed.), *Münsterischer Kommentar zum Codex Iuris
Canonici*, II, Essen, Ludgerus, losbladig, 265/2.
[35] H. FLATTEN, "Die Eheverfahren", in J. LISTL, H. MÜLLER en H. SCHMITZ (ed.),
Handbuch des katholischen Kirchenrechts, Regensburg, Friedrich Pustet, 1983, 989.
[36] Het gegeven dat in de fase die de *recursus* voorafgaat het recht op rechtsbijstand
niet bestaat, was meer concreet het voorwerp van kritiek. Zie C. GULLO, "Il ricorso gerarchico. Procedura e decisione", in A.A.V.V., *La giustizia amministrativa nella Chiesa*,
Vaticaanstad, Libreria Editrice Vaticana, 1991, 92 e.v.

Hoewel het optreden van de advocaat in de hier geschetste configuratie eigenlijk het *gevolg* is van een verstoorde band, wordt ze door de betrokken overheid vaak als de *oorzaak* ervan gezien[37]. De bisschop ervaart de advocaat dan ook als een concurrent; de advocaat ondergraaft de bisschoppelijke verantwoordelijkheid als eerste verzoener die uit diens ambt voortvloeit[38].

Tweede model:

Anders dan het eerste, accepteert het *tweede model* wel degelijk de advocaat. Aversie en defensieve reflexen blijven uit. De bisschop aanvaardt het belang van het recht op verdediging, zelfs als dat aan de orde is in de verhouding tussen een bisschop en zijn priester. Anders uitgedrukt: conflict en incardinatie hebben elk een specifiek terrein en hun eigen wetmatigheden. Alleen is het zo dat ze, in de hypothese van een relatie tussen een priester en zijn bisschop, elkaar overlappen.

Bij het tweede model rijst op dat specifieke terrein een probleem: de bisschop aanvaardt niet dat, wanneer het conflict loopt, de relatie die voortvloeit uit de incardinatie op bepaalde punten moet wijken voor de wetmatigheden van het conflict. De bisschop blijft beide wegen *tegelijkertijd* bewandelen (fig.2), wat reële conflictoplossingen bemoeilijkt en de positie van de advocaat inknelt.

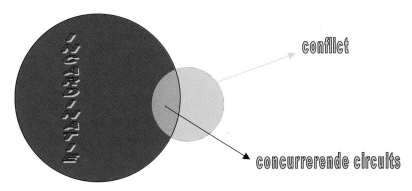

Figuur 2

[37] Een vrij negatieve perceptie van de advocaat is trouwens niet nieuw. Zie bv. A. JULLIEN, *Juges et avocats des Tribunaux de l'Église*, Rome, Officium Libri Catholici/Catholic Book Agency, 1970, 63-72.

[38] Impliciet speelt bij bisschoppen wellicht vaak de gedachte dat de advocaat dossiers waarbij het om unfaire verzuchtingen van clerici gaat, zouden moeten weigeren, indachtig wat werd geschreven door Quintillianus, *Institutiones oratoriae*, lib. XII, c. 7: "Neque defendet omnes orator, idemque partum illum eloquentiae suae salutarem non etiam piratis patefaciet, duceturque in advocationem maxime causa."

Een voorbeeld om de problematiek van de concurrerende circuits te illustreren. Een priester heeft een geformaliseerd conflict met zijn bisschop. Hij wordt, in het raam van canon 1734 als stap op weg naar een hiërarchisch beroep, samen met zijn advocaat door de bisschop ontvangen. Een pluspunt, want strikt canoniek hoeft dat in deze fase nog niet. Tijdens de sessie wordt het spel formeel correct gespeeld. Enkele dagen later nodigt de bisschop zijn priester nogmaals uit, deze keer voor een informeel gesprek in het raam van de incardinatieverhouding. Daarbij uit de bisschop zijn ongenoegen over de persoon en de aanpak van de advocaat en raadt zijn priester aan de weg van het formeel-juridische conflict te verlaten.

Het voorbeeld toont aan dat, anders dan bij het eerste model, de zelfstandigheid van de juridische procedure alsmede de eigen rol van de advocaat formeel worden erkend. Uit die erkenning worden echter helemaal geen consequenties getrokken wat de incardinatieverhouding betreft. Die wordt inhoudelijk niet in het minst beïnvloed door het lopende juridische conflict. Er is sprake van twee parallelle circuits. In het eerste, juridische circuit, heeft de bisschop een beslissend-beoordelende functie, in het tweede treedt hij op als ordinaris binnen de incardinatieverhouding. Beide verhoudingen lopen simultaan. Het diepere motief om zo te handelen, lijkt mij de theologisch geïnspireerde gedachte dat de incardinatieband op geen enkel moment verzwakt of verflauwt, ook niet wanneer een formele procedure werd opgestart.

Hoe dan ook: ofschoon beide wegen theoretisch los staan van elkaar, vertonen ze toch raakvlakken. Vooral de rol van de advocaat wordt daardoor erg kwetsbaar. Hij is immers slechts bij één van de twee circuits betrokken, terwijl de bisschop en de priester wèl een volledig overzicht behouden. De advocaat dreigt daarbij een slecht geïnformeerd randfiguur te worden, die geacht wordt te begrijpen dat hij op elk ogenblik opzij kan worden geschoven ten voordele van de sacrale incardinatieband. Dat is niet correct. Een analogie kan hier worden gemaakt met het recht waarover de advocaat beschikt om de processtukken in te kijken. Bewijzen die via een ander circuit, zoals de biecht, worden verzameld, mogen niet bij de juridische uitspraak worden betrokken[39]. Zou ook in de hypothese van interactie tussen recht van verdediging en incardinatie

---

[39] Zie bv. K.-TH. GERINGER, "Das Recht auf Verteidigung im kanonischen Ehenichtigkeitsverfahren", *Archiv für katholisches Kirchenrecht*, 1986, 438. Cf. ook F. DANEELS, "De iure defensionis brevis commentarius ad allocutionem summi pontificis diei 26 ianuarii 1989 ad rotam romanam", *Periodica*, 1990, 256-261.

niet kunnen gelden dat buiten de procedure ingewonnen bewijsmateriaal juridisch als onbestaande moet worden beschouwd?

Derde model:

Pas in het *derde model* wordt het conflict in al zijn consequenties ernstig genomen. Dat impliceert niet alleen een *autonoom bestaan* van het conflict met daarbij een belangrijke rol voor de advocaat, maar tevens een vorm van exclusiviteit. Ook wanneer het conflict zijn beslag vindt, duurt de band van incardinatie die de bisschop en de priester met elkaar hebben natuurlijk voort. Maar een facet ervan wordt opgeschort, en dit voor de looptijd van de procedure. Dit betekent dat de figuur van de incardinatie niet volledig uitwerking kan krijgen: de bisschop onthoudt zich nadrukkelijk van pastorale gesprekken op het terrein van het conflict. Bovendien is hij voorzichtig in het tot stand brengen van persoonlijke contacten, zeker wanneer die ook *in tempore non suspecto* niet gebruikelijk waren. De bisschop doet er dus alles voor om een correcte procedure niet te doorkruisen, wat onder meer betekent dat hij geen pogingen onderneemt om de advocaat buitenspel te zetten (fig.3).

Natuurlijk blijft de priester geïncardineerd. Maar een facet ervan, bepaalde contacten met de bisschop, worden opgeschort zolang de procedure loopt. Overigens hoeft zulk een strategische terugtocht geenszins te betekenen dat verzoeningspogingen en middelen om de escalatie van het conflict te vermijden, worden opgegeven. Het kerkelijk wetboek vermeldt wijzen om gedingen te vermijden (can. 1713-1716), die ook via een advocaat tot stand kunnen worden gebracht. Canon 1733 laat daarenboven in verband met het beroep tegen administratieve decreten eenzelfde klok horen. Het is zeer wenselijk, luidt het daar, dat telkens wanneer iemand zich door een decreet benadeeld acht, een betwisting tussen hem en de auteur van het decreet vermeden wordt en dat gezamenlijk naar een billijke oplossing wordt gezocht, waarbij mogelijk ook gezaghebbende personen betrokken worden om te bemiddelen en de zaak te bestuderen, zodat het geschil op een geschikte wijze wordt vermeden of opgelost. Niets belet om de advocaat te kwalificeren als zo'n gezaghebbende persoon. Canoniek is die interpretatie beslist verdedigbaar, en een beetje zin voor humor is ook in de kerk niet verboden.

Anders uitgedrukt: de bisschop neemt in dit derde model een ruimhartige houding aan tegenover het autonome conflict en tegenover de rol van

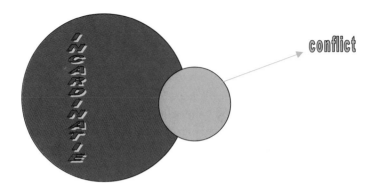

Figuur 3

de advocaat. Vooreerst vermijdt hij de introductie van parallelle circuits. Hoe? Hij schort bepaalde consequenties van de theologisch diepzinnige incardinatie op om de procedure volop een kans te geven. Vervolgens dringt hij de advocaat niet terug tot binnen de krijtlijnen van het formele conflict, een fase waarbij bisschop en priester eigenlijk al niet meer echt *on speaking terms* zijn. Neen, hij neemt ook notitie van de advocaat bij pogingen om een verdere escalatie te vermijden. Laatstgenoemde wordt op die wijze positief bij het conflict betrokken en fungeert niet langer als een schadelijke stoorzender.

Uit wat voorafgaat moge duidelijk zijn geworden dat de draagwijdte van het recht op verdediging en de rol van advocaat in het eerste model vrijwel afwezig blijven, stapsgewijs vergroten en tenslotte in het derde model echt ernstig worden genomen. Dat mijn voorkeur naar het derde model uitgaat, behoeft geen verdere argumentatie. Een situering in een ruimer kader kan evenwel nuttig zijn.

EEN TERUGBLIK, OF WAAR HET ECHT OM GAAT

De bijdrage die de lezer nu voor ogen heeft, begint met een schets van de problemen die het loutere bestaan van de functie van advocaat in de kerk enkele decennia terug leken te scheppen. Theologische opties ten aanzien van de waarheid of de plaats van de pastoraal maakten de advocaat, binnenkerkelijk dan, tot een bedreigde soort. Hij paste niet zomaar naadloos in het vreedzame canonico-theologische model. Zijn loutere aanwezigheid was een aanklacht; ze suggereerde dat binnenkerkelijke liefde grenzen kende of dat over de waarheid kon worden gemarchandeerd. Uiteindelijk haalden deze theologische bezwaren het niet en kreeg de advocaat een plaats in de Codex, waar zijn ambt betrekkelijk *low profile* tussen andere ambten en taken wordt beschreven. Tot zover het wetgevende verhaal. Maar zoals professionele canonisten maar al te goed weten: de tekst van de wet is betrekkelijk.

Pas nadat de wet tot stand kwam, geschiedde en geschiedt wat zo typisch is voor het kerkelijk recht van de laatste jaren: hoewel op macro-vlak geformuleerde theologische bezwaren tegen een bepaalde rechtsfiguur of een bepaald ambt, in casu dat van advocaat, bakzeil haalden, gaat de discussie doodgewoon verder op micro-vlak. In het geval van de advocaat betekent dit dat – binnen de wettelijke contouren van zijn naakte bestaan – moeizaam naar wegen moet worden gezocht om de positie van de advocaat te bepalen in een canoniekrechtelijke context die tevens een theologisch mijnenveld is. Bijvoorbeeld: hoe springt de advocaat om met de gedachte dat in een huwelijksproces alleen maar naar een ontologische waarheid wordt gezocht? Hoe vervult hij zijn rol in onafhankelijkheid binnen een systeem dat wegens als dwingend aangevoelde theologische redenen het principe van scheiding van machten verwerpt? De vraagstelling spitst zich in alle scherpte toe op terreinen waar eerder profane, door de Codex erkende rechtsbeginselen zoals het recht op verdediging, in aanraking komen met zuiver theologisch geïnspireerde noties zoals het incardinatiebeginsel. Op dat vlak vindt een getouwtrek plaats tussen algemene rechtsbeginselen en het handhaven van de specifieke eigenheid van de kerk. Kortom, het gaat dus bij de hier aan de orde zijnde problematiek wezenlijk om een discussie tussen recht en theologie op micro-vlak, ergens te velde. Boudweg: hoeveel doodgewoon niet-sacraal recht is aanvaardbaar binnen de veilige muren van het theologisch bepaalde instituut kerk?

Wie scherp toekijkt, merkt trouwens dat heel wat binnenkerkelijke discussiepunten van de laatste jaren precies hiermee te maken hebben. De eigenheid van de kerk en haar theologische opties gaan in de clinch met rechten of legitieme verwachtingen die vooral in het profane recht hun voedingsbodem vinden. Geen enkel ander thema verhit de binnenkerkelijke gemoederen op een vergelijkbare wijze. Geen enkele andere problematiek zet zoveel kwaad bloed. Drie voorbeelden.

De apostolische brief *Ordinatio sacerdotalis* over de priesterwijding van de vrouw (1994) stelt duidelijk dat de kerk zich niet gerechtigd acht

vrouwen tot priester te wijden[40]. Theologische principes maken derhalve
dat een maatschappelijk hoog geprezen recht, namelijk het gelijkheids-
beginsel, het veld moet ruimen. Het gaat derhalve niet om een discretio-
naire beslissing van de kerkelijke overheid. Die zou het zelf mogelijk
ook wel anders willen[41], maar acht zich gebonden door de goddelijke
ordening van de kerk[42]. Theologische basisconcepten halen het van
moderne vrijheidsrechten.

De apostolische brief *Ad tuendam fidem* (1998)[43] voegt aan de Codex
een reeds in de geloofsbelijdenis bekende nieuwe categorie van geloofs-
waarheden toe[44]. Gezien haar eminent theologisch statuut, moet de pro-
faanrechtelijk erg in de watten gelegde vrijheid van meningsuiting hiervoor wijken. Onfeilbare waarheden van de eerste en van de tweede
categorie laten vrije discussie niet toe. Dit heeft niets te maken met een
negatieve houding tegenover vrije meningsuiting, maar alles met het
overwicht van de theologisch gefundeerde waarheid ten overstaan van
moderne vrijheidsrechten[45].

De instructie over vragen betreffende de medewerking van lekengelovigen aan het dienstwerk van priesters uit 1997 schetst belangrijke theologische principes, waarbij de onvervangbare leidende rol van de priester zeer duidelijk wordt bevestigd[46]. Een neveneffect hiervan is dat de
rol van de leek in het bestuur van de kerk en in de liturgie wordt teruggedrongen. Uiteraard geschiedt dat binnen een algemene sfeer die uiterst

[40] IOANNES PAULUS PP. II, Epistola Apostolica de Sacerdotali ordinatione iuris tantum
reservanda *Ordinatio Sacerdotalis*, 22.5.1994, *AAS*, 1994, 545-548.

[41] In een recent artikel stelt een vrouwelijke auteur dat de gelijke waardigheid tussen
man en vrouw helder uit de kerkelijke documenten blijkt. Zie M.E. OLMOS ORTEGA, "La
consideración de la mujer en los documentos de la Iglesia", *Revista Española de Derecho
Canonico*, 1998, 233-254.

[42] Cf. *AAS*, 1994, 548: "... declaramus Ecclesiam facultatem nullatenus habere ordinationem sacerdotalem mulieribus conferendi (...)." Deze onbevoegdheid betekent
meteen dat op een mogelijk machtsargument geen beroep kan worden gedaan.

[43] IOANNES PAULUS PP. II, Litterae apostolicae motu proprio datae quibus normae
quaedam inseruntur in Codice Iuris Canonici et in Codice Canonum Ecclesiarum Orientalium *Ad Tuendam Fidem*, 18.5.1998, *AAS*, 1998, 458-461.

[44] Cf. hierover B.E. FERME, "Ad Tuendam Fidem: Some Reflections", *Periodica*,
1999, 579-606.

[45] B.E. FERME, *o.c.*, 606 legt duidelijk de band met Christus: "It therefore should
come as no surprise that with Ad Tuendam Fidem this vital process continues as it meets
the challenge of correctly perceiving the contours of the teaching authority of the Church,
received from Christ himself."

[46] Congregatio pro clericis et aliae, *Instructio de quibusdam quaestionibus circa fidelium laicorum cooperationem sacerdotum ministerium spectantem*, 15.8.1997, *AAS*, 1997,
852-877. Verder citeer ik de Nederlandse tekst, die op het moment van de uitvaardiging
van de instructie onmiddellijk in Vaticaanstad verscheen.

positief staat tegenover het engagement van de leek[47]. Maar een juridisch valoriseren van diens statuut mag niet tot theologische chaos leiden. Theologische principes primeren[48] dus op de ook in de Codex beschermde rechten van de leek, waaronder zijn recht op vrij initiatief.

Drie voorbeelden, drie keer voert de delicate combinatie van theologische basisconcepten en juridische beginselen tot het binnenkerkelijke overwicht van de eerste categorie. Dit illustreert naar mijn aanvoelen twee dingen. Ten eerste blijft het aan elkaar smeden van eerder profane rechtsbeginselen en aloude theologische figuren en instituten een uiterst belangrijke opdracht voor het kerkelijk recht. Ik zou zelfs zeggen: dé basisopdracht. De Codex vermeldt normen ten aanzien van elk van beide categorieën. Maar hoe die normen zich tegenover elkaar verhouden, blijft onvermeld. De dwarsverbindingen genoten nauwelijks de belangstelling van de wetgever, zij waren duidelijk voor later. En hier beland ik bij mijn tweede punt: later is nu, de universele wetgever is op dit ogenblik druk doende met het maken van die dwarsverbindingen. Keuzes, die in het verbale elan van de CIC 1983 nog uitgesteld konden worden en die dus op het macro-vlak achterwege bleven, worden vandaag gemaakt. Daarbij valt het overweldigende overwicht van de aloude theologische concepten op, waardoor de in het wetboek van 1983 nogal prominent aanwezige profane beginselen verder worden teruggedrongen. De drie hier aangehaalde voorbeelden gaan allemaal in die richting.

Uiteraard is zo'n handelwijze legitiem. Toch zou het voor vele gelovigen psychologisch bevrijdend werken om waar te nemen dat het bouwen van een brug tussen theologische principes en profane rechtsbeginselen niet altijd ten koste van deze laatste categorie verloopt. Er heerst immers bij bepaalde groepen van gelovigen een soort achterdocht – hoeft het gezegd volkomen onterecht – waarbij wordt gesuggereerd dat het overwicht van de theologische concepten een verkapte machtsgreep van de kerkelijke overheid inhoudt. Zij is immers de hoedster van de theologische orthodoxie, en beschikt daarbij over een monopolie dat in

---

[47] Cf. *Instructie over vragen betreffende de medewerking van lekengelovigen aan het dienstwerk van de priesters*, Vaticaanstad, Libreria Editrice Vaticana, 1997, 8: "We moeten met tevredenheid constateren, dat zich in vele particuliere Kerken de medewerking van niet gewijde gelovigen aan het pastorale dienstwerk van de clerus op een zeer positieve wijze ontwikkelt."

[48] *Instructie...*, 13: "Wezenlijk voor de katholieke leer over de Kerk is het feit dat het ambtelijk priesterschap gefundeerd is in de apostolische opvolging: dit ambt continueert de zending die de apostelen van Christus ontvangen hebben."

het geval van behoorlijke rechtsbescherming in ieder geval minder uit-gesproken is. Zoals al gezegd: achterdocht is ongerechtvaardigd. De ker-kelijke overheid wordt uiteraard niet door machtsoverwegingen geleid. Toch kunnen het recht op verdediging en de rol van de advocaat een merkwaardige voorbeeldfunctie vervullen. Zij slagen er mogelijk in aan te tonen dat bij het maken van de delicate dwarsverbinding tussen theo-logische en juridische concepten, deze laatste niet per definitie het onderspit moeten delven. Immers, in het in deze bijdrage beschreven derde model worden bepaalde consequenties van de incardinatie opge-schort, zonder dat door deze werkwijze het op zichzelf uiterst waarde-volle instituut van de incardinatie ook maar een ogenblik in het gedrang wordt gebracht. Het blijft natuurlijk onverkort bestaan. Wél is het zo dat de incardinatie, binnen de configuratie van het concrete conflict, een stapje terug moet zetten ten voordele van het recht op verdediging en de rol van de advocaat. Zonder theologische principes te schaden, wordt in dit concrete geval voorrang gegeven aan een profaan-juridisch georiën-teerd algemeen rechtsbeginsel. Een dergelijke benaderingswijze zal door vele sceptici van vandaag als hoopgevend worden ervaren, en komt de geloofwaardigheid van het canonieke rechtssysteem ongetwijfeld ten goede. Een gevaarlijke gedachte wordt ontzenuwd, namelijk de idee dat de kerk alleen maar in theorie de moderne mensenrechten waardeert, omdat deze laatste op het terrein telkenmale weer op ondoordringbare theologische veto's botsen. Het complexloos accepteren van zowel de tussenkomst als het behoorlijke functioneren van de advocaat zijn van onschatbare waarde. Voor mensen die in een moderne rechtstaat zijn opgegroeid, staat de advocaat symbool voor het recht op verdediging en voor reële onafhankelijkheid. Zelfs in een instituut zonder evenwicht van machten blijft het mogelijk om, met enige verbeeldingskracht, de advocaat ernstig te nemen. Het binnenkerkelijke effect dat hiermee gepaard gaat, mag niet worden onderschat. Het bevestigt een aloude gedachte: creatief kerkelijk recht is nooit uitzichtloos. En het is evenmin een *contradictio in terminis*.

THE ADVOCATE IN THE CHURCH. SOURCE OF CONFLICT OR CONFLICT SOLVER?

RIK TORFS

PREHISTORY: THE ADVOCATE BETWEEN COUNCIL AND CODE

How the Church should be defined is a professional matter for accomplished theologians. That the Church aims to be, among other things, a community of believers, and that this notion has in principle a positive connotation, is something that few would want to deny. There prevails, then, a positive atmosphere in the Church – theologically it could hardly be otherwise. Conflict, and the lawyers that are invariably associated with conflict, would seem to be out of place here. There has always been an acute sense of this tension, whereby the advocate's role in canon law is – structurally, as it were – the subject of continual discussion.

Of course, rosy images arouse suspicion. Perfection is impossible. The French-Romanian writer, E. M. Cioran, was convinced of that: "Le paradis n'était pas supportable, sinon le premier homme s'en serait accommodé.[1]" And yet, during the period between the Vatican II council and the promulgation of the new code (1965-1983), it was the tension between the church as a harmonious community of believers, on the one hand, and the advocate's position, associated with conflict, on the other, that stood in the way of any enthusiastic attitude toward the advocate in canon law.

Whoever devoted any consideration to ecclesiastical advocates at that time always had matrimonial law in the back of his mind, for this was the domain *par excellence* in which process law manifested itself. And it was this fact that provided two additional reasons for being particularly wary when dealing with advocates and their antics.

First of all, a matrimonial procedure seeks, at least in theory, nothing else than to uncover the truth[2]. And there is but one of these. Whereas it

---

[1] The quote is from *De l'inconvénient d'être né*, published in Paris by Gallimard in 1973. It was included in his collected works, E. M. CIORAN, *Œuvres*, Paris, Gallimard Duarto, 1999, 1278.

[2] Cf. IOANNES PAULUS PP. II, *Ad Tribunalis Sacrae Romanae Rotae Decanum, Praelatos Auditores, Officiales et Advocatos, novo Litibus iudicandis ineunte anno: de veritate iustititiae matre*, 4.2.1980, *AAS*, 1980, 172-178, 174: "Tutti gli atti del giudizio

is not uncommon that the parties in a civil divorce procedure sharpen
their knives in order to be proved right, in an ecclesiastical procedure,
they are in search of the truth. It is even possible that both parties share
exactly the same point of view, believing that the marriage is null due,
for example, to *metus reverentialis*, a fear inspired by respect. Indeed, a
matrimonial procedure has a declaratory, not a contradictory, character[3].
There are no genuine conflicts of interest between the parties, which is
why an advocate is essentially superfluous – so goes an argument that is
frequently invoked, especially by theologians. Of course, this sort of rea-
soning is not really persuasive: even though the truth is central, the way
in which it is uncovered, with all of the wounds that such a search can
inflict, in itself justifies the presence of an advocate[4]. Some believers
would even choose an audacious *non constat de nullitate* above the triumph of a humiliating truth in which they do not recognize themselves.
And whether there are *really* no conflicting interests in a matrimonial
procedure will be discussed in a moment. But in any event, the advocate's role will at the very least appear different in the context of marriage law in the Church than in a purely secular context, which goes
some way to making understandable the skepticism that was, in the past,
so characteristic of the role of the advocate.

The second argument against the advocate takes a step further. It goes
as follows: not only is the canon annulment procedure not a matter of a
contentious dispute, the whole case is actually not even a legal question.
The tribunal's approach to the matter must be essentially pastoral[5].
Judges and auditors, often priests with extensive experience in the field,
are perfectly well equipped to provide strong pastoral support without
other parties – advocates for instance, cool servants of the law – having

---

ecclesiastico, dal libello alle scritture di difesa, possono e debbono essere fonte di verità
(...)." Cf. also K. HARTELT, "Liebe und Recht. Anmerkungen zur theologischen Grundlegung des Kirchenrechts", in K. LÜDICKE, H. PAARHAMMER and D.A. BINDER (ed.), *Recht
im Dienste des Menschen. Eine Festgabe Hugo Schwendenwein zum 60. Geburtstag*,
Graz, Styria, 1986, 328.

[3] A. JACOBS, *Le droit de la défense dans les procès en nullité de mariage*, Paris, Éditions du Cerf, 1998, 438; 509.

[4] R. TORFS, "Le droit de la défense dans les procès en nullité de mariage. Quelques
réflexions à propos d'un livre d'Ann Jacobs", *Revue de droit canonique*, 1998, 45 ff.

[5] Cf. P.J.M. HUIZING, "Schets voor herzien canoniek huwelijksrecht", in J.H.A. VAN
TILBORG, TH.A.G. VAN EUPEN and P.J.M. HUIZING, *Alternatief kerkelijk huwelijksrecht*,
Bilthoven, Amboboeken, 1974, 37-53. On p. 37 Huizing begins like this: "The following
sketch does not intend to be a complete draft for a new canonical marriage law, but only
an initial schematic outline for an exchange of ideas about the direction in which canonical marriage law, with pastoral orientation, might further develop."

to get involved. To the contrary: their awkward questions would disturb the momentum. What some ecclesiastical courts provided in the Seventies and Eighties was a purely pastoral approach, which was then squeezed, post factum, into a procedural framework simply *pour les besoins de la cause*[6]. What the parties involved experienced as pastoral talks were defined *retrospectively* as, say, the interrogation of one party by the judge. I know of a Dutch pastor who is a staunch proponent of divorce celebrations, where everyone can have a good cry[7] under the good-natured guidance of the pastor. Such an approach was, and is, irreconcilable with canonical marriage law. It is also losing ground. Privacy is important today[8], and the idea that complete openness about all aspects of life is required in order to unveil every matrimonial mystery is an idea in retreat. Nowadays. But in the period from 1965 to 1983, when there was a kind of legal vacuum within the church, the seeming irreconcilability between a "pastoral" procedure and the advocate's contribution was regularly felt in all its intensity.

In spite of the two arguments just adduced against any role for advocates in canon law, more specifically in matrimonial law, the advocate is granted a place in the code of 1983. The accent is still on advocacy in the light of matrimonial law[9], but there is also mention of advocates, among other places[10], in oral contentious trials (can. 1663-1664), penal procedure (can. 1723 and 1725) and, what will likely be very important in the future, hierarchical recourse (can. 1738). The simple fact that the advocate is turning up at all in the codex, and this in various places, has in a single stroke changed the field of discussion. The question is no

[6] Sometimes such things took place in a brilliant way. Cf. O.F. TER REEGEN, "La jurisprudence hollandaise", *Revue de droit canonique*, 1990, 167-178.

[7] Cf. L. GOERTZ, "Kerkelijke rechtbanken aan het einde van hun Latijn? Scheiden zonder juridisch gesol", *de Bazuin*, September 5, 1997, 4-6. The sob session turns up on p. 5. On the same page, Goertz writes: "In the legal sense, an ecclesiastical court seems to me (...) unnecessary. But I do see another, new task for the court: to provide pastoral advice to individual couples and pastors who would like more help from a higher level in the difficult questions of human relations."

[8] Privacy is protected in the code of canon law as well, namely in canon 220. On this point, see, for example, A. CAUTERUCCIO, "Il diritto alla buona fama ed alla intimità. Analisi e commento del can. 220", *Commentarium pro religiosis*, 1992, 39-81.

[9] The advocate is forbidden, however, in the *ratum sed non consummatum* procedure. Cf. canon 1701 §2. On this, see H. PREE, "Die Rechtsstellung des advocatus und des procurator im kanonischen Prozeßrecht", in W. AYMANS and K.-TH. GERINGER (ed.), *Iuri Canonici Promovendo. Festschrift für Heribert Schmitz zum 65. Geburtstag*, Regensburg, Friedrich Pustet, 1994, 315-318.

[10] For more details about the special categories of advocates and cases, see C.P. PEÑARROYA, *Abogados y procuradores en la Curia Romana*, Rome, E.V., 1996, 432 p.

longer: "is there a place for advocates in the church?" Henceforth the question presents itself differently: "*how* does the advocate fit into the church's legal system?" "How is he integrated into a subculture not immediately his own?" The next question is quite a bit more thorny: "in what way does the advocate interact with legal ideas having strong theological overtones, such as the principle of incardination?" The right to defence and incardination – the concepts do not sit very easily with each other, just as gluttony is inappropriate for a mystic, or irony is opposed to the serious profession of canonist.

THE ADVOCATE IN THE LEGAL SYSTEM OF THE CHURCH

The advocate enjoys recognition in canon law. The profile is sketched out in canon 1483. He must have attained the age of majority[11] and must be of good name. According to a declaration of July 12, 1993, by the Apostolic Signatura, this good name is lacking for an advocate living in a so-called *irregular relationship*[12]. In addition, he must be Catholic[13], unless the diocesan bishop allows otherwise. He must be a doctor in canon law, or a genuine expert in some other way. Finally, he must be approved by the bishop[14]. From this list, it appears that the bishop has a great deal of leeway not to accept the advocate. Even if he is a Catholic doctor in canon law, he can still be banished to the desert if, in the bishop's opinion, he is not of good name. Moreover, the same bishop can refuse to grant his approval without having to give any further

---

[11] The age of majority is eighteen years. Cf. canon 97 §1.

[12] Cf. "Acta Tribunalium S. Sedis. Supremum Signaturae Apostolicae Tribunal. Prot. N 24339/93 V.T.", *Periodica*, 1993, 699-700. In his commentary, Raymond Burke takes a broad view of the consequences of this irregular relationship: "... qui vivit in unione irregulari ad exercendum munus advocati admitti nequit. Hoc principium, quatenus generale, per se valet pro advocato ad casum admittendo, pro advocato in albo advocatorum inscribendo, et pro advocato iam in albo inscripto." The right to privacy, clearly, is overruled.

[13] Klaus Lüdicke believes it is advisable (*angemessen*) that the advocate has not left the church by a formal act. See K. LÜDICKE, "Prozeßrecht: Parteien", in K. LÜDICKE, (ed.), *Münsterischer Kommentar zum Codex Iuris Canonici*, V, Essen, Ludgerus, loose leaf, 1483/2. Strictly speaking, this is not a requirement. But in combination with the required oath (can. 1454) and the great degree of discretion that the diocesan bishop exercises in approving the advocate, Lüdicke's got the right general idea as far as practice is concerned.

[14] This takes place by decree. Cf. H. PREE, "Die Rechtsstellung ...", in W. AYMANS e.a. (ed.), *o.c.*, 305: "Die Approbation gilt nur für das Gericht des approbierenden Bischofs. Einer zusätzlichen Bestellung durch den Vorsitzenden des kirchlichen Gerichtshofes bedarf es nicht."

reasons[15], and if this happens tacitly, no hierarchical appeal is possible. Once he is accepted, the advocate must also take an oath[16].

The essential difficulty regarding the advocate's position, however, does not lie here. Who the advocate is plays a part of course, but how he is able to go about his work is much more essential. What is decisive is the more theoretical question, but a question with very practical consequences, concerning what role an advocate can *really* fulfill in a system that does not accept the principle of the separation – or to call it by a more modern name: the *balance*[17] – of powers. In our Western democracies, we are not accustomed to such a question. What is clear is that the advocate's role varies according to the different concrete ecclesiastical situations in which he must act. In a number of areas, the advocate's role will not be much different from what would be expected of him in civil law; in other areas, however, the difference will be palpable at every moment[18]. With respect to the role of the ecclesiastical advocate, a distinction must be drawn between three different domains:

(1) The ordinary *contentious trial* between two parties differs very little in the church from the discussion in secular law. This is because, in such conflicts, the theological relevance is rather marginal or entirely absent. Moreover, the ecclesiastical authority is not one of the parties to the action. These two factors mean that the weight of the case remains limited. Some examples might help to illustrate this. An argument over a bequest, over a benefice, or over certain consequences of a contract – on the assumption that such cases are submitted to an ecclesiastical court, which is not so frequent given the more immediate results usually produced by purely secular procedures – have two things in common: not much is at stake theologi-

---

[15] J. Weier asks for more precise norms regarding the bishop's approval: J. WEIER, "Der Anwalt im kirchlichen Eheprozeß. Neue Bestimmungen im CIC", in A. GABRIELS and H. J. F. REINHARDT (ed.), *Ministerium Iustitiae. Festschrift für Heribert Heinemann*, Essen, Ludgerus, 1985, 408. Concerning the advocate's participation in hearings, stricter norms for refusing an advocate are demanded by J. WEIER, "Die Parität zwischen Ehebandverteidiger und Anwalt im kirchlichen Ehenichtigkeitsprozeß - Erreichtes und Erwunschtes", *De processibus matrimonialibus*, 1997, 333.

[16] See canon 1454. Cf. on this point also H. PREE, "Die Rechtsstellung ...", in W. AYMANS e.a. (ed.), *o.c.*, 305.

[17] Cf. W.J. WITTEVEEN, *Evenwicht van machten*, Zwolle, Tjeenk Willink, 1991, 100 p.

[18] H. PREE, "Die Rechtsstellung ...", in W. AYMANS e.a. (ed.), *o.c.*, 313-314 distinguishes three objectives of legal assistance, namely (1) expert assistance in the dialectic of the proceedings; (2) to seek a convergence between formal and material truth; (3) the economy of the procedure, i.e., the expectation that the suit proceeds *citius, melius ac minoribus sumptibus*.

cally, and the ecclesiastical authority is not a party to the action. The result is clear: in such a contentious action, the advocate has possibilities at his disposal which are very much like those a secular lawyer would have in a similar situation.

(2) The *matrimonial process* occupies a middle position. On the one hand, it is characterized by the theological specificity of marriage law in the Church. This has already been mentioned earlier: think of the declaratory character of the procedure. The procedure must necessarily limit itself to investigating the validity of the marriage, since dissolution is rejected on theological grounds. In this area, then, the advocate has to accommodate himself, and he will play a role that would be unavailable to him in secular law. The tug-of-war leading to a favourable divorce settlement gives way to a scrupulous quest for an ontological truth, if not in practice then at least from a theoretical point of view. How amicable can the advocate come across to his client, when he is part of such a process of uncovering the truth? Where do his ultimate loyalties lie? Clearly not in the same place as for a secular lawyer. Some advocates identify quite strongly with their specifically ecclesiastical roles and write a plea in which, unbeknownst to their client, they actually argue against him in the name of the truth[19]. This is a particular risk in an advocate who sees himself as very pastoral, and who believes this quest for truth will have a healing effect on his client. Others will accept the principle of discovering the truth, without necessarily assigning the main role to themselves: seeking the truth is all very well, but even then a party has need of a proper defence[20]. Ultimately, it is up to the court to assume its responsibility. In

---

[19] That the advocate is indeed permitted to argue in favour of his client is evident from the allocutio mentioned in note 2, from Pope John-Paul II. In *AAS*, 1980, 175, one can read: "Ad aiutare quest'opera delicata ed importante dei giudici sono ordinate le 'defensiones' degli Avvocati, le 'animadversiones' del Difensore del Vinculo, l'eventuale voto del Promotore di Giustizia. Anche costoro nello svolgere il loro compito, i primi in favore delle parti, il secondo in difesa del vinculo, il terzo in 'iure inquirendo', devono servire alla verità, perché trionfi la giustizia." A similar openness is also shown in *Communicationes*, 1984, 64 ff.

[20] In a number of countries, the advocate only enters the picture in an appeal. See, on this point, L. ZIMMERMANN, "Die Mitwirkung des Anwalts im kanonischen Eheprozeß. Praktische Erfahrungen und Anregungen", in R. PUZA and A. WEISS (ed.), *Iustitia in caritate. Festgabe für Ernst Rößler zum 25jährigen Dienstjubiläum als Offizial der Diözese Rottenburg-Stuttgart*, Frankfurt am Main/Berlin/Bern/New York/Paris/Vienna, Peter Lang, 1997, 447. It is obvious that, in this case, adequate legal assistance is more important than pastoral help. Had the latter been central, the advocate would probably have already been contacted for the procedure in the court of first instance.

short, the theological specificity of the matrimonial procedure forces the advocate to adapt his strategy, and perhaps also his spiritual temperament[21]. On the other hand, it is equally true that in a matrimonial procedure, the ecclesiastical authority is not an immediate party to the action. This idea, of course, demands some qualification. Zenon Grocholewski sees the annulment procedure as a genuine lawsuit in which the partner who requests annulment is the plaintiff and the church itself, represented by the *defensor vinculi*, functions as defendant. Grocholewski considers the *conventus* as an intervening third party, in the framework of canon 1596[22]. Not everyone agrees with this. Lüdicke sees the matrimonial procedure, correctly in my view, as a judicial affirmation of a *factum iuridicum*[23]. But even if one accepts Grocholewski's idea on a theoretical level, it does not yet entail any practical involvement on the part of the ecclesiastical authority. Granted, marriage has not only an individual[24], but also a public significance[25]. However, the ecclesiastical authority as such does not consider itself to be directly addressed by the lawsuit. This has a calming effect and also explains why, with respect to marriage cases, the ecclesiastical authority seldom gets very worked up.

(3) Penal procedure and hierarchical recourse with the possibility of appealing to an administrative court[26] take a step further. Now the

---

[21] Cf. S. GHERRO, "Il diritto alla difesa nell'ordinamento canonico", *Monitor Ecclesiasticus*, 1988, 2, refers quite strongly to the specificity of matrimonial law. The link between *giusto* and *vero* is not so simple: "L'affermazione trova peculiare riscontro quanto alle cause matrimoniali, giacché, tramite le medesime, si persegue esclusivamente *l'accertamento* di un *quid* che rileva nell'ordine giuridico degli uomini, ma che implica contemporanea incidenza in quello soprannaturale dei rapporti con la Divinità."

[22] Z. GROCHOLEWSKI, "Quisnam est pars conventa in causis nullitatis matrimonii?", *Periodica*, 1990, 357-391.

[23] K. LÜDICKE, "Der kirchliche Ehenichtichkeitsprozeß. Ein processus contentiosus?", *Österreichisches Archiv für Kirchenrecht*, 1990, 299. Against Grocholewski's view, see also R. AHLERS, "Der Stellenwert des Verteidigungsrechtes im Ehenichtigkeitsverfahren", *De processibus matrimonialibus*, 1995, 289. With regard to the defence of the matrimonial relationship, she says: "Er schützt das öffentliche Interesse der Kirche und tritt für die Gültigkeit der Ehe ein, er personifiziert diese aber nicht."

[24] In a decree coram Agustoni of March 17, 1976 one reads that cases that are in both the private and the public interest, such as a matrimonial trial, the advocate restricts himself to defending the private interests of parties. On this, see G. ERLEBACH, *La nullità della sentenza giudiziale 'ob ius defensionis denegatum' nella giurisprudenza rotale*, Vatican City, Libreria Editrice Vaticana, 1991, 230.

[25] R. AHLERS, *o.c.*, 289.

[26] Legal assistance is possible as *pars resistens* and as *pars recurrens*. Cf. Z. GROCHOLEWSKI, "L'autorità amministrativa come ricorrente alla Sectio Altera della Segnatura Apostolica", *Apollinaris*, 1982, 770-779.

authority is indeed involved in the suit: as judge, as administrator, as a party. Moreover, this occurs, as already mentioned, in a context that creates some uncertainty since the separation or balance of powers does not exist – a fact which is itself based on theological assumptions, such as the theological position of the bishops as successors to the apostles, and the Pope as successor to Peter. Yet even if the existing context is clear, even if it might be theologically inevitable, that does not mean the situation is any less precarious. How can an advocate be of any use in procedures, such as hierarchical recourse, where a bishop involved in a conflict with his priest is both a judge and a party to the suit, at least from the viewpoint of secular law? To give a concrete example: if, in the context of canon 1734, an advocate requests a bishop to revoke or emend his own decree, it is perhaps best not to do this by emphasizing the legal errors it contains. The bishop would likely find such an argument less than persuasive. The advocate will usually attempt to find a pragmatic way out, in full awareness of his inferior position. In a state of affairs where someone is asked to judge his own administrative decision, it is probably advisable to substitute a strictly legal plea by a well considered and balanced petition. The mutual entanglement of administrative power and judging authority means that a businesslike, legalistic approach runs the risk of being counter-productive.

So much for the three categories. The division of the working domain of an ecclesiastical advocate into three different sub-groups can be graphically represented by three circles:

The *outer circle* shows the procedures in the first category. The problematic is not, or barely, theologically significant and the church authority is not a party to the action.

The *middle circle* contains procedures that are theologically significant, but the church authority is not, as such, involved in the action. The advocate must make a mental adjustment, but still has a great deal of procedural leeway.

The *inner circle* combines a theologically significant case with a more or less direct involvement of the church authority. The advocate finds himself in a quite uncertain position, and regularly resorts to semi-juridical negotiation strategies.

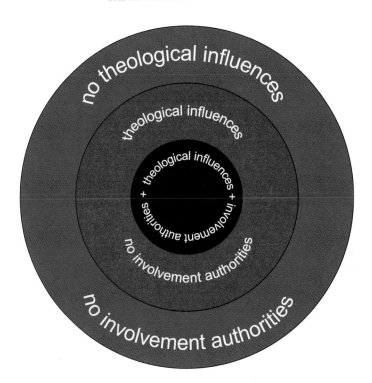

	no theological influences
	no involvement authorities

	theological influences
	no involvement authorities

	theological influences
	+
	involvement authorities

The closer one gets to the centre of the diagram, the more atypical the advocate's role becomes. In a system without a balance of powers, how can the advocate continue to fulfill as independent a role as possible as he moves towards the inner circle? The code of canon law does not really address this question, and that, in my view, is positive. Too much text would expose possible contradictions without being able to resolve them. The particular legislator would also do well to show restraint, especially when his legislation goes so far as to limit, in the name of streamlining, the advocate's ability to function and his radius of action[27]. When an advocate who must already operate from a structurally weak position[28] is also confronted with a diocesan status, his position threatens to become very shaky indeed, for the legislator who imposes the norms of a strict status is identical with the administrator who proclaimed a decree, and identical with the authority who can revoke or emend this decree. A diocesan status only makes the symbiosis of the powers more complete. Theologically, everything is perfectly in order, but from a juridical viewpoint it is still oppressive.

But let us get back to the diagram and its consequences. To the extent that the inner circle comes closer, the legal guarantee of a substantial and qualitative right to defence becomes more problematic. At the same time, the advocate's task gets more difficult. Very quickly, the discussion begins to hinge on the truth, and the judging authorities are not in a position where they could easily take some distance. At the level of "hard law", the level of legal guarantees, not much can be done to remedy this. Theological demands, especially if they are based on divine law, take precedence over mere legal norms that guarantee a fair distribution of rights or try to give shape to the right of defence. Whoever practises canon law simply has to accept this *rebus sic stantibus*, whatever he might think of it in the depths of his heart. Yet even though legal guarantees along the lines of those in democratic constitutional states are impossible, some *non-binding guidelines* could still be developed, which the church authorities could then freely take up in their function as legislator/administrator/judge. I would place the emphasis on "freely". There is absolutely no obligation, unless one considers canon 221 and the due process principles as formally superior norms, also within the

[27] Additional requirements for an appointment, apart from the requirement of universal law, can also act as hindrances. Cf. F.J. RAMOS, "Considerazioni sulla necessità dell'intervento degli avvocati nei processi di dichiarazione di nullità del matrimonio canonico", *Ius Ecclesiae*, 1998, 290.
[28] For instance, he is not yet at the same level as the defender of the matrimonial bond.

church. I think that still is the way to the future[29]. At the same time, however, it must be admitted that the formal supremacy of the Christian believers' rights and duties with respect to other legal norms is given partial support in legal theory[30], but is certainly not universally accepted or applied by the practitioners of canon law. Yet even without this legally grounded formal superiority, some *non-binding guidelines* would help to promote the plausibility of the system of canon law. Let us leave it at that, at least for now.

In the next section, I would like to develop a guideline for the hard core of the system, for cases in the very innermost circle. As an example, I will take a very concrete case in which theological concepts and figures are in full play, and where the ecclesiastical authorities are even party to the action: a real minefield for the advocate, that much is certain.

THE ADVOCATE IN THE INNER CIRCLE

More often than in the past, conflicts between a priest and his bishop assume formal, legal dimensions, and they set out on the path of hierarchical recourse. Not infrequently, this choice is made after other forms of dialogue between the parties have been exhausted. In this perspective, the formalization of their difference of opinion is felt to be a last resort. This evolution towards greater juridification is not entirely surprising. Although the relationship between priest and bishop is supported by the principle of incardination, this purely ecclesiastical relationship no longer protects the *dramatis personae* from external influences. The internal process of socialization that priests are submitted to is less comprehensive than in the past. The priest's personality no longer dissolves completely into his vocation: he is also a consumer, a citizen – in a certain sense even an employee, though this would be unacceptable in a healthy vocational theology. The consequences of this are clear: more and more conflicts are formalized. But getting back to the specific moment of this formalization: it is not an easy time. There is a great deal

---

[29] I have worked out this idea elsewhere, including during a lecture held in Weingarten on November 27, 1997 entitled *Die Menschenrechte, die Grundrechte der Christen und das Kirchenrecht*. The text is in press. Also in press is the text of a seminar held in Minneapolis on October 5, 1999 entitled *Rights in Canon Law: Real, Ideal or Fluff?*

[30] See R. PUZA, "Der Rechtsschutz im Kirchenrecht zwischen Hierarchie und Grundrechten", *Theologische Quartalschrift*, 1999, 179-194.

of irritation. The priest has recourse to an advocate because the tradi-
tional dialogue situation between priest and bishop has not had the
desired result.

The formal, legal situation is located alongside another, theologically
elaborate legal idea, namely incardination[31]. Canon 265 imposes incardination on every cleric[32], and the cleric is required to respect and obey his
ordinary (can. 273). From the other side, the ordinary, for example the
diocesan bishop, must provide *honesta sustentatio*, decent support[33] and
social assistance, according to the law (can. 384).

The situation just sketched is thus rather complex. And the question
that is really the essential one is this: what can the advocate possibly do
in a formalized conflict between two people who are condemned,
through incardination, to deal with each other, but who just cannot man-
age to? The question is so complex because two sharply different principles are related here, without any common factor to bring them
together. On one side there is the legal procedure and the right to
defence, so two legal concepts; on the other side there is the principle of
incardination, a theologically well-founded legal idea which, because of
its intrinsic depth, should render superfluous any formal legal conflict.
But this is precisely the problem: it "*should* render superfluous". What
is undesirable from a theological viewpoint – a formal legal conflict –
nevertheless occurs. This fact alone is often a source of irritation to the
authority involved. Which is understandable, since the formal escalation
of the conflict can be seen as partly the result of his own failings. The

---

[31] Pope John-Paul II provides additional information in the post-synodal exhortation
Pastores dabo vobis from March 25, 1992. See IOANNES PAULUS PP. II, Adhortatio apostolica postsynodalis ad Episcopos, Sacerdotes et Christifideles totius Catholicae Ecclesiae, de Sacerdotium formatione in aetatis nostrae rerum condicione *Pastores dabo vobis*,
25.3.1992, *AAS*, 1992, 657-804. In nr. 31, p. 707-709, it is stressed that incardination is
more than simply a legal connection. It also produces spiritual and pastoral consequences.

[32] On this point, see, for instance, J.I. DONLON, "Incardination and Excardination: The
Rights and Obligations of the Cleric and of the Church – A Matter of Pastoral Justice",
in Canon Law Society of America (ed.), *Proceedings of the Fifty-third Annual Convention*, Washington, CLSA, 1992, 124-153. On p. 131 Donlon writes: "This provision of
the law, a near restatement of the 1917 Code, is in keeping with the oldest traditions of
the church. Underlying this norm are two reasons. First, no individual should be inducted
into the clerical state unless there is a need in the community for his service. As John
Lynch points out in the CLSA commentary, 'private devotion, honor, and convenience
are not sufficient justification for ordination.' Second, the institute of incardination
expresses a concern for stability within the ranks of the clergy."

[33] H. SCHMITZ, "Die Sustentation der Kleriker", in H. PAARHAMMER (ed.), *Vermögensverwaltung in der Kirche. Administratorum bonorum. Oeconomus tamquam paterfamilias. Sebastian Ritter zum 70.Geburtstag*, Thaur/Tirol, Echter, 1988, 177-191.

question then is: how can the principle of incardination and the unique role of the advocate in the formalized conflict be brought together in an acceptable way? There are three possible models. Since they are not in any way qualitatively equivalent, I will not present them here in the form of a juxtaposition. Rather, there is a gradation beginning with the first, qualitatively weak model, and ending with the third model, in which the right of defence and the role of the advocate are taken seriously, even within the context of incardination.

First model

The first model accepts the principle of incardination as the exclusive departure point for further action. Completely in line with canon 384, the bishop protects the rights of his priests, who are his assistants and advisers. A conflict between the partners in an incardination relationship cannot, of course, be absolutely ruled out, but it must be situated entirely within the limits of the incardination (fig. 1). How does such an attitude become apparent? The bishop can, for example, refuse to have a discussion with a priest in the presence of an advocate, because the advocate's presence would disrupt the purity of the incardination relationship[34]. Heinrich Flatten once wrote, with reference to matrimonial procedure, that the presence of an advocate in a hearing could possibly act as an inhibition to the parties involved[35]. By analogy one could argue that the advocate might cause similar inhibitions in the framework of the incardination relationship. He hinders an open dialogue between two people who are more closely tied to each other than simply by a legal relationship – so the argument might go. Indeed, canon 1738 states that the one making a recourse has the right to call on an advocate, but before such a formal recourse exists, there is not yet any such right. This means that the bishop technically has the right to refuse any intervention by an advocate until the recourse has been submitted – a rule that Carlo Gullo rightly objects to, but one that is nevertheless in the code for everyone to read[36].

---

[34] Klaus Mörsdorf qualified incardination as 'geistlichen Heimatverband'. This terminology has something domestic about it. On this, see also H.J.F. REINHARDT, "Volk Gottes: die Kleriker", in K. LÜDICKE (ed.), *Münsterischer Kommentar zum Codex Iuris Canonici*, II, Essen, Ludgerus, loose leaf, 265/2.

[35] H. FLATTEN, "Die Eheverfahren", in J. LISTL, H. MÜLLER and H. SCHMITZ (ed.), *Handbuch des katholischen Kirchenrechts*, Regensburg, Friedrich Pustet, 1983, 989.

[36] The fact that the right to assistance does not exist in the phase preceding the *recursus* has been an object of criticism. See C. GULLO, "Il ricorso gerarchico. Procedura e decisione", in A.A.V.V., *La giustizia amministrativa nella Chiesa*, Vatican City, Libreria Editrice Vaticana, 1991, 92 ff.

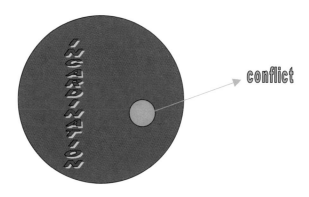

Fig. 1

It is not uncommon for the bishop to associate a recourse with a rift in the relation of trust between the priest and himself. In short, the example just given exhibits no constructive connection between incardination and formal conflict. The conflict must be talked out within the relationship of trust imposed by incardination. It is that simple.

Though the advocate's presence in the situation outlined here is actually the *consequence* of a disrupted relationship, it is often seen as the *cause* of disruption by the authority involved[37]. The bishop will then experience the advocate as a competitor: the advocate undermines the bishop's responsibility to be the initial conciliator, a responsibility deriving from the bishop's office[38].

Second model

In contrast to the previous one, the second model does indeed accept the advocate. Aversion and defensive reflexes are left behind. The bishop accepts the importance of the right to defence, even if it is in question in the relationship between a bishop and his priest. In other words, conflict and incardination each have their own specific terrain

---

[37] A somewhat negative perception of the advocate is nothing new. See A. JULLIEN, *Juges et avocats des Tribunaux de l'Église*, Rome, Officium Libri Catholici/Catholic Book Agency, 1970, 63-72.

[38] Perhaps the bishops often implicitly believe that advocates should decline cases dealing with unfair complaints by clerics, bearing in mind what Quintilian wrote: *Institutiones oratoriae*, lib. XII, c. 7: "Neque defendet omnes orator, idemque partum illum eloquentiae suae salutarem non etiam piratis patefaciet, duceturque in advocationem maxime causa."

and their own rules. It is just that they happen to overlap, in the case of a conflict between a priest and his bishop.

In the second model, a problem arises in that specific area: when there is a conflict, the bishop will not accept that the relationship based on incardination must give way, on certain points, to the rules of the conflict. The bishop continues along both paths *at the same time* (fig. 2), making much more difficult any real solution to the conflict as well as complicating the position of the advocate.

Let me give an example to illustrate this problem of the competing circuits. A priest has a formalized conflict with his bishop. In the framework of canon 1734, he and his advocate are received by the bishop as a step on the way to a hierarchical recourse. This is positive, since strictly canonically, that is not yet necessary at this stage. During this audience, the formal rules are correctly observed. A few days later, the bishop invites his priest once again, this time for an informal chat in the framework of the incardination relationship. On this occasion, the bishop expresses dismay with the advocate personally and with his approach, and he advises his priest to abandon the path of the formal, legal conflict.

This example shows that, contrary to the first model, here the independence of the legal procedure and the specific role of the advocate are formally recognized. This recognition, however, leads to absolutely no consequences regarding the relationship of incardination, which is not in the least influenced by the ongoing legal conflict. One could describe it as two parallel circuits. In the first, legal circuit, the bishop's role is to decide and to pass judgement; in the second circuit, he acts as an ordinary within the incardination relationship. Both relationships are maintained simultaneously. The underlying motive for acting in this way seems to be the theologically inspired idea that the relationship of incardination is never, at any moment, weakened or stressed, not even when formal procedures are initiated.

In any event however, although the two avenues are theoretically distinct from each other, they do have some contact points. This makes the role of the advocate, in particular, quite vulnerable, since he is involved in only one of the two circuits, whereas the bishop and the priest both have a complete overview. The advocate runs the risk of being a poorly informed, marginal figure, one who is presumed to understand that he can be shunted aside at any moment for the sake of the sacred incardination relationship. This is not correct. An analogy can be drawn here with the advocate's right to view the documents relating to the case. Evidence

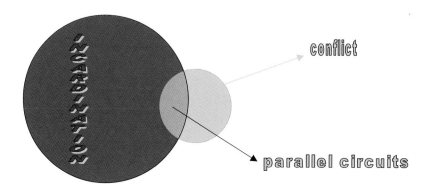

Fig. 2

that has been collected through another circuit – the confessional for instance – cannot be involved in the legal decision[39]. In the hypothetical case of an interaction between incardination and the right to defence, might it not also be advisable that evidence collected outside the procedure must be considered as legally non-existent?

Third model

It is only in the third model that the conflict, in all its ramifications, is taken seriously. This implies not only the *autonomous existence* of the conflict, with an important role for the advocate, but also a form of exclusiveness. The incardination link between bishop and priest continues, even when the conflict is settled. But one aspect of it is suspended for the length of the procedure. This means that all the consequences of incardination cannot be fully exercised: the bishop explicitly refrains from having pastoral discussions in the area of the conflict. He is also cautious in cultivating personal contacts, especially when they were not usual ones *in tempore non suspecto*. The bishop does everything in his power, then, not to derail a correct procedure, which also means that he makes no attempts to sideline the advocate (fig. 3).

Of course, the priest is still incardinated. But one aspect of this, i.e., certain contacts with the bishop, are suspended for as long as the procedure

---

[39] See, for instance, K.-TH. GERINGER, "Das Recht auf Verteidigung im kanonischen Ehenichtigkeitsverfahren", *Archiv für katholisches Kirchenrecht*, 1986, 438. See also F. DANEELS, "De iure defensionis brevis commentarius ad allocutionem summi pontificis diei 26 ianuarii 1989 ad rotam romanam", *Periodica*, 1990, 256-261.

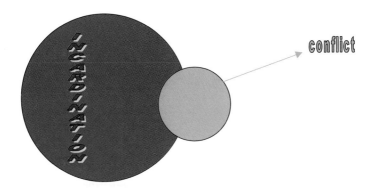

Fig. 3

lasts. This kind of strategic withdrawal does not mean that reconciliation attempts and means of avoiding an escalation of the conflict are abandoned. The code of canon law mentions methods of avoiding a trial (can. 1713-1716), and these can also be initiated by an advocate. In addition, canon 1733 says similar things in connection with recourse against administrative decrees. It is highly desirable, the text says, that whenever someone feels injured by a decree, a contention between that person and the author of the decree should be avoided, and a common and fair solution should be sought, where possible with the involvement of persons in authority who can mediate and study the affair, in such a way that the disagreement is avoided or solved in an appropriate manner. Nothing prevents the advocate from being qualified as just such a person in authority. In canon law, such an interpretation can certainly be defended, and a sense of humour is not forbidden in the church either.

   To put it another way, in this third model the bishop adopts a benevolent attitude towards the autonomous conflict and towards the advocate's role. First of all, he avoids the introduction of parallel circuits. How? He suspends certain consequences of theological incardination in order to give the procedure a proper chance. Then, rather than forcing the advocate to work within the boundaries of the formal conflict, a phase in which bishop and priest are actually no longer on real speaking terms, he also recognizes the advocate in his attempts to prevent further escalation. In this way, the advocate is involved in the conflict and no longer functions as merely a harmful nuisance.

From what has just been said, it should be clear that the scope of the right to defence, and the role of the advocate, are practically non-existent in the first model, and gradually expand until, in the third model, they are taken quite seriously. That my own preference is for the third model requires no additional argumentation, but it might be useful to situate it within a broader context.

A RECAPITULATION, OR WHAT IT IS REALLY ALL ABOUT

The text you are now reading began by sketching the problems apparently associated, a few decades ago, with the very existence of the function of advocate in the church. Theological choices regarding truth, or the place of pastoral work, made the advocate, at least in the Church, a species under threat. He did not fit seamlessly into the peaceful canonical-theological model. His mere presence was an accusation, suggesting that love within the church had limits or that one could bargain about the truth. Ultimately these theological objections lost ground and the advocate acquired a place in the code, where his office was given a relatively low profile, among other offices and tasks. So much for the legislative story. But as professional canonists know all too well, the text of the law is relative.

Only after the law was established, something quite typical of canon law in recent years occurred, and is still occurring: although the theological objections formulated at the macro level against a specific legal idea or a specific office came to nothing, at the micro level the discussion simply continued. In the advocate's case this means that – within the legal contours of his mere existence – a way must be found to determine the advocate's position in a legal context which is also a theological minefield. For instance, how does the advocate handle the idea that a matrimonial procedure only seeks an ontological truth? How does he carry out his role independently within a system that rejects the principle of the separation of powers because of theological reasons felt to be binding? The problem becomes most acute in areas where more secular legal principles – e.g., the right of defence – though recognized by the code, nevertheless clash with theologically inspired notions such as the principle of incardination. At this level there is a tug-of-war between universal legal principles and the maintenance of the church's own specificity. In short, what is really at stake in the problematic described here is essentially a dispute between law and theology at the micro level. To put it bluntly, how much ordinary, non-sacred law is acceptable within the secure walls of the theologically determined institution of the Church?

The attentive observer will have noticed that a good number of the debates in the church in recent years were about precisely this point. The church's specificity and theological choices fight it out with rights or legitimate expectations whose main breeding ground is secular law. No other topic is able to heat up emotions in the church to a comparable degree. No other problematic creates so much ill will. Three examples.

The apostolic letter *Ordinatio sacerdotalis* (1994) about the ordination of women to the priesthood[40] clearly states that the church does not consider itself entitled to ordain women. In the name of theological principles, then, a right which is highly valued in society, namely the principle of equality, must give way. And this is not a matter of a discretionary decision made by the ecclesiastical authority, who might possibly have wanted it otherwise[41], but who feels constrained by the divine order of the church[42]. Fundamental theological concepts win out over modern rights of freedom.

The apostolic letter *Ad tuendam fidem* (1998)[43] adds to the code a series of new categories of religious truth, already familiar from the profession of faith[44]. And because of their eminent theological status, the right to freedom of expression, so favoured by secular law, must bow down to them. Infallible truths of the first and second category tolerate no free discussion. This has nothing to do with a negative attitude towards freedom of expression, but everything to do with the priority of a theologically grounded truth over modern rights of freedom[45].

---

[40] IOANNES PAULUS PP. II, Epistola Apostolica de Sacerdotali ordinatione iuris tantum reservanda *Ordinatio Sacerdotalis*, 22.5.1994, *AAS*, 1994, 545-548.

[41] In a recent article, a female author states that the equal dignity of men and women emerges clearly from the church documents. See M.E. OLMOS ORTEGA, "La consideración de la mujer en los documentos de la Iglesia", *Revista Española de Derecho Canonico*, 1998, 233-254.

[42] Cf. *AAS*, 1994, 548: "... declaramus Ecclesiam facultatem nullatenus habere ordinationem sacerdotalem mulieribus conferendi (...)." This lack of competence has the direct consequence that the whole debate can not be about power.

[43] IOANNES PAULUS PP. II, Litterae apostolicae motu proprio datae quibus normae quaedam inseruntur in Codice Iuris Canonici et in Codice Canonum Ecclesiarum Orientalium *Ad Tuendam Fidem*, 18.5.1998, *AAS*, 1998, 458-461.

[44] On this point, see B.E. FERME, "Ad Tuendam Fidem: Some Reflections", *Periodica*, 1999, 579-606.

[45] B.E. FERME, *o.c.*, 606 makes a clear link with Christ: "It therefore should come as no surprise that with Ad Tuendam Fidem this vital process continues as it meets the challenge of correctly perceiving the contours of the teaching authority of the Church, received from Christ himself."

The instruction (1997) concerning questions about the collaboration of laypeople with priests outlines some important theological principles, and very clearly reaffirms the irreplaceable leading role of the priest[46]. A side-effect of this is that the layperson's role in the governance of the church, and in the liturgy, is diminished. Of course, all this occurs within a more general sphere that is extremely positive about the layperson's engagement[47]. But a legal valorization of the layperson's status may not lead to theological chaos. Once more, then, theological principles prevail[48] over the layperson's rights protected in the code, including his right to free initiative and to promote his own undertakings.

Three examples, and three times the delicate combination of theological concepts and legal principles leads, in the church, to a predominance of the former. In my view, this illustrates two things. First of all, the fusing together of more secular legal principles with ancient theological ideas and institutions remains an extremely important task for canon law. I would even say: the fundamental task. The code mentions norms with regard to both categories, but how these norms relate to each other is not mentioned. These cross-connections attracted scant attention from the legislator; clearly they were for later. And this brings me to the second point: later means now. The universal legislator is at this very moment busy making these cross-connections. The choices that were postponed in the verbal exuberance of the 1983 code, and that were thus omitted from the macro level, are today being made. What is striking is the overwhelming weight given to the ancient theological concepts, whereby the secular principles that were so prominent in the code of 1983 are pushed further back. The three examples I gave here all move in this direction.

This way of working is of course legitimate. But it would be psychologically emancipating for many faithfull if they could see that building a bridge between theological principles and secular legal principles is not always at the cost of the latter. There exists among certain groups of believers a kind of suspicion – entirely unjustified, it must be said – in

[46] Congregatio pro clericis et aliae, *Instructio de quibusdam quaestionibus circa fidelium laicorum cooperationem sacerdotum ministerium spectantem*, 15.8.1997, *AAS*, 1997, 852-877.
[47] *Ibid.*, 854: "Gaudenter quidem animadvertimus in compluribus Ecclesiis particularibus fidelium non ordinatorum cooperationem in ministerio cleri pastorali perquam efficaciter agi, …"
[48] *Ibid.*, 858: "Praecipuum caput doctrinae ecclesiologicae catholicae est ut fundamenta ponantur ministerii ordinati in successione apostolica ex eo quod ministerium hoc missionem producit quam Apostoli a Christo receperunt."

which it is suggested that the weight given to theological concepts is a kind of disguised *coup d'état* by the church authorities, since they are the guardians of theological orthodoxy and there enjoy a monopoly which is less pronounced in the case of adequate legal protection. As I said, such suspicion is unjustified. The church authorities are not guided by considerations of power. And yet, the right of defence and the role of the advocate can fulfill a singular function as examples, for they can demonstrate that, in constructing the delicate cross-connections between theological and legal concepts, the latter do not necessarily have to come off worst. Indeed, in the third model described above, certain consequences of incardination are suspended without ever bringing for a single moment the valuable institution of incardination under threat. Obviously, it continues to exist unimpaired. It is simply that, within the bounds of the concrete conflict, incardination must take a step back for the benefit of the right to defence and the role of the advocate. Without damaging the theological principles, in this concrete case preference is given to a universal legal principle, oriented towards secular law. Such a method for approaching the matter will be seen by many skeptics today as a sign of hope, and it undoubtedly strengthens the credibility of the canonical legal system. And a dangerous idea is deflated, namely the idea that the church values modern human rights only in theory, because these rights always clash with an impenetrable theological veto when applied in the field. To accept, without any qualms, both the intervention and the proper functioning of an advocate is of inestimable value. For people who have grown up in a modern state characterised by the rule of law, the advocate stands as a symbol of the right to a defence, as well as for real independence. Even in an institution lacking any real balance of powers, it is still possible, with a bit of imagination, to take the advocate seriously. The effect that this has within the church should not be underestimated. It reaffirms an ancient idea: creative canon law is neither a hopeless delusion nor a *contradictio in terminis*.

AT THE CROSSROADS OF TWO LAWS:
SOME REFLECTIONS ON THE INFLUENCE OF SECULAR LAW ON THE CHURCH'S RESPONSE TO CLERGY SEXUAL ABUSE IN THE UNITED STATES

JOHN P. BEAL

I. INTRODUCTION

During the past fifteen years, public and highly publicized complaints of sexual abuse of minors by Catholic priests have become a distressingly familiar feature of the ecclesial landscape in the United States.[1] It may be hyperbolic to claim, as Andrew Greeley has, that the phenomenon "may be the greatest scandal in the history of religion in America and perhaps the most serious crisis Catholicism has faced since the Reformation."[2] Nevertheless, these complaints, some spurious but all too many well founded, have been costly to the Church-financially costly, of course, but spiritually costly as well.

These revelations and their repercussions have forced the Church in the United States to adopt a more aggressive approach to preventing and dealing with clergy sexual abuse. In developing this new approach, the Church has had to be attentive to both secular and canon law. On the one hand, the Church has had to ensure that its manner of dealing with clerics and complaints of clerical misconduct does not expose it to liability for negligence under civil tort law; on the other hand, the Church has had to accept the limits imposed by canon law on its options for dealing with the problem. Finding a balanced approach that complies with both laws has not been easy. The time allotted for this lecture does not permit a thorough and systematic analysis of the impact of this problem on the Catholic Church in the United States. I would, however, like to explore how the intersection of American law and canon law has shaped the Church's approach to dealing with sexual abuse of minors by clerics.

---

[1] See Philip Jenkins, *Pedophiles and Priests: Anatomy of a Contemporary Crisis* (New York: Oxford University Press, 1996) 33-142. For a more journalistic, but somewhat tendentious overview, see Jason Barry, *Lead Us Not Into Temptation: Catholic Priests and the Sexual Abuse of Children* (New York: Doubleday, 1992).

[2] Andrew M. Greeley, "Forward," in Jason Berry, xiii.

II. THE CHURCH BEFORE AMERICAN LAW

Understanding the context within which church authorities have had to work out their new approach to clergy sexual abuse requires a grasp of some basic principles governing Church-State relations in the United States. The framework for the Church's status before secular law is established by the First Amendment to the Constitution, which stipulates that "Congress shall make no law respecting an establishment of religion, or prohibiting the free exercise thereof."[3] What has emerged from two hundred years of jurisprudence applying the First Amendment's "establishment" and "free exercise" clauses to concrete cases is a system of "separation of church and state." On the one hand, the "free exercise" clause of the First Amendment guarantees the Catholic Church, like all other religious individuals and institutions, freedom to organize itself and to pursue its religious mission without governmental interference, except when such intervention is necessitated by what the Supreme Court has called "a compelling governmental interest."[4] On the other hand, the "establishment clause" of the First Amendment has entailed that neither the Catholic Church nor any other religious organization can look to the government for financial support, privilege, or enforcement of its doctrinal or disciplinary decisions. Between Church and State, there is what Thomas Jefferson termed "a wall of separation."

As a result, the Catholic Church in the United States has had the opportunity to structure and govern itself in accord with canon law without undue governmental entanglement. This freedom from entanglement

---

[3] U.S. CONST. amend. I. Although this amendment was originally intended as a restriction only on the authority of the Congress of the United States, its principles were indirectly applied to the several states through their eventual incorporation into most state constitutions. Moreover, decisions of the United States Supreme Court have interpreted the "due process" and "equal protection" clauses of the Fourteenth Amendment to the Constitution, adopted in 1868, as applying the First Amendment's restrictions on Congress directly to the states.

[4] A "compelling government interest" is analogous to what Vatican II called "the just requirements of public order." *DH*, §4. See also *DH*, §7: "Furthermore, society has the right to defend itself against possible abuses committed on pretext of freedom of religion. It is the special duty of government to provide this protection. However, government is not to act in an arbitrary fashion or in an unfair spirit of partisanship. Its action is to be controlled by juridical norms which are in conformity with the objective moral order. These norms arise out of the need for effective safeguard of the rights of all citizens and of peaceful settlement of conflicts of rights. They flow from the need for an adequate care for genuine public peace, which comes about when men live together in good order and in true justice. They come, finally, out of a need for the proper guardianship of public morality. These matters constitute the basic components of the common welfare: *they are what is meant by public order.*" Emphasis added.

with secular government has, however, come at a price. Since the "establishment" clause of the First Amendment prevents the Catholic Church, or any other religious entity, from enjoying privileged status before the law, American law treats the Church as a private, voluntary association. Thus, the law does not recognize the claim of the Church and its subsidiary units to be moral or juridic persons and their interaction with the surrounding society is governed not by public law but by private law. One consequence of the Church's private law status is that its dioceses, parishes and institutional apostolates do not enjoy immunity from civil suits for damages resulting from the tortious actions and omissions of its ministers and employees.[5]

Although the courts have generally considered clerics to be "employees" of the Church, they have refused to apply the doctrine of *respondeat superior* to hold the Church vicariously liable for the sexual abuse of minors by its clerics. Even when the cleric used his office or ministry to gain access to young people and the abuse was perpetrated on church property, the courts have consistently held that sexual relations between priests and members of the faithful cannot be considered within the "scope of their employment."[6]

Nevertheless, the Church has sometimes been found to be liable for damages suffered by the victims of such sexual abuse because of its negligence in hiring, retaining or supervising clerics or because of its failure to fulfill its duty to warn others about their sexual proclivities. The Church can be held liable for damages because of its negligence even for activities outside their agents' or employees' scope of employment, if it knew or should have known about their propensity for misconduct (i.e., it was "on notice") but failed to exercise reasonable care to prevent it.

---

[5] The Church and other charitable organizations had once been protected from tort claims by the judge-made doctrine of "charitable immunity." However, in 1942 a federal court rejected the doctrine. President and Directors of Georgetown College v. Hughes, 130 F. 2d 810 (D.C. Cir. 1942). This decision was followed by a spate of similar decisions until the doctrine of charitable immunity had been abolished in virtually every jurisdiction. William W. Bassett, "Christian Rights in Civil Litigation: Translating Religion into Justiciable Categories," *The Jurist* 46 (1986) 232-237.

[6] On the one hand, such misconduct cannot be said to be "either required by or instant to a priest's duties." Milla v. Tamayo, 232 Cal.Rptr 685, 690 (Cal.App. 2 Dist, 1986). On the other hand, while it might be said that such misconduct was in some absolute sense foreseeable, to bring the activity within the scope of employment, "the foreseeable event must be characteristic of the activities of the enterprise" and "it would deny every notion of logic and fairness to say that sexual activity between a priest and a parishioner is characteristic of the Archbishop of the Roman Catholic Church." Ibid.

Many courts have been reluctant to decide whether ordaining a man whom church officials knew or should have known had molested minors in the past and who offended again after ordination constitutes negligent hiring. Since such a determination would require the court to examine church doctrine and law to establish what makes a person suitable for ordination, these courts have held that the First Amendment bars such examinations.[7] Other courts have not seen the First Amendment as an insuperable bar to judging whether the Church was negligent in "hiring" a priest.[8] These courts have contended that they can make a judgment about negligence on the basis of religiously neutral, secular principles and without reference to church doctrine. Thus, in a 1997 case, a Texas trial court held a diocese liable for nearly $120 million in damages, in part, because the jury found that, prior to a priest's ordination, the diocese had negligently ignored information that he had been sexually involved with adolescent boys.[9] More common than negligent hiring and retention cases have been cases in which church authorities were aware of a priest's sexual attraction to young people because of previous complaints but, nonetheless, reassigned him to ministry where he offended again. In these cases, courts have sometimes found, on the basis of neutral, secular standards, that the Church was negligent in its efforts to supervise the delinquent cleric or failed to fulfill its duty to warn.

III. NEW APPROACHES AND SOME QUESTIONS

The discovery that hundreds of young people have been molested by Catholic priests is itself sufficient impetus for church authorities to tighten their approach to screening candidates for ordained ministry and to dealing with clerics accused of sexual abuse of minors. The Church must do what it can to protect young people from sexual abuse. However, the willingness of the secular courts to find dioceses and religious institutes liable for damages resulting from their negligence in hiring, supervising and retaining sexually abusive clerics has given church authorities a compelling financial motive for a more aggressive approach

---

[7] Byrd v. Faber, 565 N.E. 2d 584 (Ohio 1991); Schieffer v. Catholic Archdiocese of Omaha, 244 Neb. 715, 508 N.W. 2d 907 (1993); Bladen v. First Presbyterian Church, 857 P.2d 789 (Okla. 1993); Pritzlaff v. Archdiocese of Milwaukee, 533 N.W. 2d 780 (Wis. 1995); Isley v. Capuchin Province, 880 F.Supp. 1138 (E. D. Mich. 1995).

[8] Kenneth R. v. Roman Catholic Diocese of Brooklyn, 654 N.Y.S. 2d 791 (A.D. 2 Dept. 1997); Nutt v. Norwich Roman Catholic Diocese, 921 F.Supp. 66 (D. Conn. 1995).

[9] John Doe, et al. v. Rev. Rudolph Kos, No. 93-0528-G (Dallas Dist. Ct. 1997).

to screening candidates for ordained ministry and to disciplining delinquents.

I would like to devote particular attention to two problematic practices of particular concern to canonists: 1) the use of increasingly invasive methods for screening candidates for ordained ministry and the extension of these methods to those already ordained; and 2) efforts to distance dioceses and religious institutes from abusive clerics, including removing them from the clerical state. Both of these practices have been prompted by misperceptions of the requirements of American law for dealing with clerical misconduct and oint to the need for those who serve the Church to be conversant with both canon and secular law.

A. Psychological Testing and Other Breaches of Privacy

The Church has long been concerned that candidates for ordained ministry be "capable of dedicating themselves permanently to the sacred ministry in light of their human, moral, spiritual, and intellectual characteristics, their physical and psychological health and their proper motivation" (c. 241, §1). Since the physical and psychological [*psychica*] state of health [of candidates] must generally be examined by medical experts and others who are experienced in the psychological sciences,"[10] those responsible for seminary admissions have routinely employed psychological testing to assess the suitability of candidates.[11] As the number of reports of sexual abuse of minors by clerics mounted, cries arose for even more careful and invasive screening of candidates for seminary admission.[12] Often submission to psychological testing and willingness to release the results of this testing to those responsible for external forum decisions has become a prerequisite for admission to seminaries and to ordination. Moreover, admissions procedures have also begun to include quite explicit questions about the candidate's sexuality. For

---

[10] Sacred Congregation for Catholic Education, *Ratio fundamentalis institutionis sacerdotalis*, AAS 62 (1970) 349.

[11] National Conference of Catholic Bishops, *The Program of Priestly Formation*, 4th edition (Washington: United States Catholic Conference, 1992) §517: "Seminary administrators should consider psychological assessment and integral part of admission procedures." See also Paul L. Golden, "The Formation of Clerics," in *The Code of Canon Law: A Text and Commentary*, ed. James Coriden, Thomas Green, and Donald Heintschel (New York: Paulist Press, 1985) 182: "Most seminaries in the English-speaking world require... a written report containing the results of psychological testing."

[12] Stephen J. Rossetti, *A Tragic Grace: The Catholic Church and Child Sexual Abuse* (Collegeville, MN: Liturgical Press, 1996) 64-67.

example, among the questions asked as part of the admissions interview at one major seminary are: "Can you briefly describe how you understand your sexual history and your sexual development?" and "We require a two year period of chaste celibate living before a person enters the seminary. Can you tell us the last time you were sexually active and what type of activity you engaged in?"

Concern for careful screening has not been limited to candidates for seminary admission. Rather, this screening has in some places been extended to those already ordained.[13] Thus, in some dioceses, all members of the presbyterate as well as extern priests working in the diocese have been asked (actually "required" as a condition for "continued employment") to submit to fingerprinting and criminal background checks and to credit checks. In one diocese, all clerics were asked to sign a "covenant of responsible service" in which they acknowledged the impropriety of a variety of behaviors including "driving under the influence of alcohol or drugs, rape, pederasty, exhibitionism, voyeurism, contributing to the delinquency of a minor, impregnation of a woman or being impregnated outside of wedlock whether a consenting adult or not, sexual harassment, the embezzlement of funds, and the like" (sic). In addition, they were asked to aver in writing that they had never heretofore engaged in such behaviors "except as noted on the back of this form" and that they would notify the diocese if they engaged in them in the future.

The policies of many dioceses (sometimes subtly) require priests accused of sexual abuse of minors and sometimes those suspected of other forms of misconduct to undergo a thorough psychiatric evaluation at an in-patient facility and to release the results to the bishop and his advisors. When priests resist such forced psychiatric examinations or refuse to release their results to church authorities, they are sometimes ordered to comply with these requirements under the obligation of clerical obedience and under threat of penal sanctions.

The stated intent of these efforts at screening present and future church ministers is to weed out sexual abusers and other miscreants and thereby prevent their harming others, especially the vulnerable. However, should a civil suit arise, these invasive background checks also provide documentation to support the claims of dioceses and religious institutes that they had done everything within their power to screen

---

[13] Some of these methods of screening have also been employed when hiring or making decisions about retaining lay church employees as well.

their ordained ministers, and therefore, that they were not negligent in placing them in ministry. Nevertheless, these investigative tactics come perilously close to breaching – if, indeed, they do not actually breach – the right to privacy (c. 220).[14]

The Church has, of course, recognized the usefulness of psychological testing and evaluation for screening candidates for ordained ministry and religious life and for assessing suitability for continued ministry.[15] It has, nevertheless, set clear limits on the permissibility of such testing and evaluation. In a little publicized 1976 instruction to pontifical representatives, the Secretary of State insisted:

1) It is not licit for anyone, either a religious or a diocesan superior, to enter into the psychological or moral intimacy of a person without having received from that person a prior, explicit, informed and absolutely free consent; in this sense, therefore, all psychological-projective or other practices, which are in fact used during the admission or continuation in Seminaries or Novitiates, are to be considered illicit if the prior and free consent of the interested party is lacking, which consent cannot be extorted in any manner.

2) Moreover, a psychologist must not manifest to a third person, whatever may be the authority with which the person is invested, both religious and political, knowledge concerning the intimate life, both psychological and moral, which he may have arrived at without the free consent of the interested party.[16]

While the instruction explicitly mentions abuses of the right to privacy in the context of seminary and religious formation, the instruction expressly extends these principles to efforts to mandate psychological

---

[14] See Alfonso Cauteruccio, "Il diritto alla buono fama ed alla intimità: Analisi e commento del canone 220," *Commentarium pro Religiosis* 73 (1992) 39-81; Viktor Papez, "Das Recht der Ordensleute auf Schutz der eigenen Intimsphäre und ihre Respektierung durch die Oberen," *Antonianum* 71 (1996) 35-55; Marcelo Daniel Colombo, "El examen psicológico de admisión y la protección de la intimidad (c. 220)," *Annuario Argentino de Derecho Canónico* 3 (1996) 129-168; Vittorio Marcozzi, "Indagini psicologiche e diritti della persona," *La civiltà cattolica* 127 (1976) 541-551; id., "Il diritto alla propria intimità nel nuovo Codice di Diritto Canonico," *La civiltà cattolica* 134 (1983) 573-580.

[15] Gregory Ingels, "Protecting the Right of Privacy When Examining Issues Affecting the Life and Ministry of Clerics and Religious," Paper presented at the annual meeting of the Canadian Canon Law Society, Vancouver, British Columbia, October 19-21, 1999, 9-13.

[16] Secretariate of State, "Instruction of the Secretariate of State with Indicative Notes," August 6, 1976, P.N. 311157.

evaluations for those already ordained as well.[17] These principles have also been applied by the Roman congregations when they have decided recourses against administrative sanctions inflicted on priests for their refusal to undergo evaluations or to release the results of such assessments to their ecclesiastical superiors.[18] In these cases, the instruction has been cited as legal authority for holding that, while ecclesiastical authorities can discipline priests on the basis of their external behavior, if it so warrants, they cannot do so merely on the basis of their refusal to cooperate in psychological evaluations. Thus, a diocesan bishop concerned about a pastor's erratic behavior can suggest that the pastor seek a psychological assessment, but he cannot compel the pastor to do so against his will. The bishop can, however, use the pastor's documented behavior as the basis for removing him from office and for refusing to reassign him until he completes an appropriate program of therapy.[19]

Whatever their usefulness in detecting potential sexual offenders may be, requiring psychological testing or evaluation or the release of the results of such testing as a condition for seminary admission or ordination or for continuance in ministry is a violation of the right of privacy, unless the subjects' prior, informed and free consent has been secured. The Vatican instruction, approvingly citing a United Nations document, even notes that, when psychological testing "is presented as a necessary pre-condition or even is simply 'recommended' or said to be 'desirable' for recruitment or for maintaining a position or getting a promotion, there is evident doubt whether the person who undergoes such tests does so voluntarily."[20] Thus, church authorities must rely on their persuasive powers to convince potential subjects of psychological testing that it is in their own best interests to consent to it.

Requiring prospective and actual ordained ministers to report their own immoral behavior to ecclesiastical authorities, as the previously mentioned questions for candidates for seminary admission and "covenant of responsible service" do, is also a violation of the right to privacy. However, such requirements also constitute a forbidden inducement to a manifestation of conscience (c. 630, §5). This prohibition on requiring manifestations of conscience is found in the section of the code dealing with religious. However, by speaking of such abuses as occur-

---

[17] Ibid.
[18] See Ingels, 7-9.
[19] Ibid.
[20] Secretary of State, Instruction. See United Nations, "Respect de la vie privée et de l'intégrité et de la souveraineté des Nations," N. E, CN.4 116.

ring "*especially* in novitiates and seminaries,"[21] the Vatican instruction extends this prohibition to all interactions between church authorities and their subjects. In fact, it was concern that such abuses of privacy were occurring even beyond the context of seminary and religious formation that prompted the inclusion of the right of privacy among the rights of all the Christian faithful in the revised code (c. 220).[22]

The apparent conflict between respect for the right of privacy and the desire to shield the Church from costly negligence judgments raises a question: will church authorities expose the Church to costly tort judgments for negligence if, in accord with canon law, they respect the right to privacy by using psychological testing and evaluation only with the free and informed consent of its subjects and refraining from other invasive screening techniques? It is impossible to answer that question with certainty, but preliminary indications are that it will not. For church authorities to be found negligent in a clergy sexual abuse case, it has to be demonstrated that they knew or should have known of a cleric's proclivities and failed to do what a reasonable person would do to prevent his offenses. If church authorities *could* only have known of his propensities by psychological testing or other methods that were violative of his privacy, it cannot be claimed that they "*should* have known" about them. That at least is the position of one California court[23] which held a "diocese had no legal obligation to provide background checks or psychological testing where the diocese had no notice of previous problems, because the individual priest's right of privacy must be respected."[24] If this decision is followed by other courts, respect for the right of privacy in screening candidates for ministry and continuance in ministry will not result in the Church being found negligent, unless church officials had evidence that they were prone to misconduct.

B. Removal from the Clerical State

Once church authorities become aware that a cleric has sexually molested minors, usually through receipt of a founded accusation, they

---

[21] Ibid." Emphasis added.

[22] Cauteruccio, 52-60.

[23] Roman Catholic Bishop of San Diego v. Superior Court, 50 Cal.Rptr. 2d 399 (Cal.App., 4th Dist. 1996).

[24] William W. Bassett and Patrick T. Shea, Legal Liability of Ecclesiastical Organizations for Personal Injuries Caused by Clergy: Committee Report (Washington: CLSA, 1999) 15-16.

are "on notice" about his proclivities. Thus, the law requires them to deal with the priest in a responsible manner. Failure to do so may result in liability for negligence. It has become the new conventional wisdom that the first response to a founded complaint of sexual abuse is to remove the accused priest from active ministry and, with his free and informed consent of course, to refer him for psychological evaluation and, if indicated, treatment. In recent years, there has been hopeful clinical evidence that priest offenders, especially those whose offenses were relatively few and with older adolescents, can be rehabilitated so that they no longer represent serious threats to the vulnerable.[25] However, no amount of therapy can guarantee that a priest will never offend again. As a result, if the cleric is returned to ministry and does offend again, the diocesan bishop or religious superior cannot claim that he was not "on notice" about the priest's problem. If there are further incidents of abuse, church authorities may be found to have been negligent, unless they can show that they acted responsibly in reassigning such a priest to and supervising him in ministry.

Thus, when priest offenders have successfully completed treatment programs, diocesan bishops and religious superiors face difficult decisions about whether to reassign them to public ministry. The faithful have expressed grave reluctance and, at times, hostility to the return of sex offenders to their communities (as evidenced by the passage of so-called "Megan's laws" in several states), much less to their parishes.[26] The days when a priest offender could be quietly reassigned to ministry without notifying the congregation are over. Unless church authorities have alerted the community of the priest's past history of abuse, they can be found to have failed to honor their duty to warn should the priest offend again.[27]

As a result of the difficulty in finding parish communities willing to accept a priest with a history of sexually abusing minors and of the fear of liability judgments in case of recidivism, many priest offenders remain on the margins of ecclesial life after treatment, still priests but denied active ministry. Some, of course, are willing to seek rescripts

---

[25] See Frank Valcour, "The Treatment of Child Sexual Abusers in the Church," in *Slayer of the Soul: Child Sexual Abuse and the Catholic Church*, ed. Stephen J. Rossetti (Mystic, CT: Twenty-Third Publications, 1991) 45-66 and Stephen J. Rossetti, *A Tragic Grace*, 87-91; L.M. Lothstein, "Can a Sexually Addicted Priest Return to Ministry After Treatment? Psychological Issues and Possible Forensic Solutions," *The Catholic Lawyer*, 34 (1991) 89-115.

[26] See Stephen J. Rossetti, *A Tragic Grace*, 81-85, 91-93.

[27] Moore v. St. Joseph Nursing Home, 184 Mich.App. 766, 459 N.W. 2d 100 (1990).

from the Holy See releasing them from the clerical state; but others resist the process of "laicization," often hoping against hope that they will be returned to ministry in the future. Thus, they remain in statuses that are difficult to categorize canonically. They are priests incardinated in their dioceses or religious institutes, but they are "retired," on "leaves of absence," or on "administrative leave," the last a canonically flawed attempt to expand the circumstances in which the restrictions that can be imposed on the accused in the course of the penal process (c. 1722) to include situations when no penal process is in prospect.[28] Some of these unassigned priests receive pensions or other forms of support from their places of incardination; others support themselves, in whole or in part, from secular employment.

Bishops and religious superiors were reasonably content to tolerate this canonically muddled situation as long as they felt confident that secular courts would consider the Church liable for negligent supervision of its ministers only for tortious conduct in which priests engaged as "agents" or ministers of the Church and not for conduct in which they engaged as "private persons." It was thought that the courts would consider a priest who had been refused an assignment to an office or ministry to be acting as a "private person" and not as an agent of the Church. Therefore, the diocese or religious institute to which an unassigned priest belonged would not be considered liable for negligent supervision of him, if he offended again.[29]

This tolerance for ambiguity began to erode in 1988 when a court in the state of Washington issued a decision that some have wrongly interpreted as holding a diocese liable for the torts of one of its priests even though he was without ministerial assignment and suspended *a divinis*. The case involved a priest of the Diocese of Lafayette, Louisiana, whose vicar general had arranged for him to live with the Jesuit community in Spokane, Washington, while the priest awaited trial for sexual abuse of minors in Louisiana. During the priest's time in Washington State, the diocese paid him a monthly stipend or subsidy, covered his living expenses, and paid his medical, counselling and legal expenses. There were also numerous other contacts between the diocese and the priest during his time in Washington. In 1985, the priest obtained employment as a drug and alcohol counsellor in the adolescent care unit of a Spokane hospital. The diocese was aware of his employment, but not that it

---

[28] See John P. Beal, "Administrative Leave: Canon 1722 Revisited," *Studia canonica* 27 (1993) 293-320.

[29] See Bassett and Shea, 7-16.

involved adolescents. In due time, the priest moved on to another hospital from which he was fired in January of 1986 "because of complaints of sexual abuse by former patients" of both hospitals.[30]

Nine of the priest's victims sued him, the two hospitals, the Diocese of Lafayette, and others. The diocese sought summary judgment on the ground that the Washington State court lacked jurisdiction to adjudicate a case involving a corporation located in the state of Louisiana. The trial court granted the motion for summary judgment but was reversed on appeal. The appellate court stated clearly that "the only issue on review is whether there is jurisdiction over the Diocese" by the Washington court[31] and that "the issue of whether the Diocese was in fact negligent in supervising Father Fontenot or whether it should have warned Deaconess or Compcare must be resolved by the trier of fact."[32] Nevertheless, the court's careful reconstruction of the contacts between the Diocese and the priest while he was in Washington and particularly its conclusion that "the duty of obedience which Father Fontenot owed the Diocese encompassed all phases of his life and correspondingly the Diocese's authority over its cleric went beyond the customary employer/employee relationship"[33] was seen, in some circles, as ominous. The Compcare decision led some lawyers to fear that, when the diocese was "on notice" about a priest's proclivities, the mere fact that he was still an incardinated cleric at the time of his new offense could now be sufficient basis for a finding of negligent supervision of its "agent" by his diocese.

This fear is based on an erroneous reading of the decision, but it has had profound repercussions for the way in which church officials are dealing with priest offenders. As a result of this fear, many diocesan bishops have thought it prudent to distance themselves and their dioceses as much as possible from offending priests, including, where feasible, effecting their removal from the clerical state. When a cleric is unwilling to petition for a rescript of departure from the clerical state from the Holy See, effecting his removal from the clerical state is a difficult undertaking. The only realistic option recognized by the code is the infliction of the penalty of dismissal from the clerical state through the judicial penal process (c. 1425, §1, 2, a).

---

[30] John Does 1-9 v. Compcare, 763 P.2d 1237, 1239-1241 (Wash.App. 1988).
[31] Ibid., 1239.
[32] Ibid., 1242.
[33] Ibid., 1242.

1. Resignation or Termination from the Office of Priest

To obviate the need for such a process, some have suggested that, when a priest is willing, he should tender to his bishop or major superior a resignation from his "office as a priest" and, if he is not willing to resign, the bishop or major superior should send him notice of his termination from "employment as a priest."[34] This approach is based on the supposition that the diocese's potential liability for negligence arises from its acts (such as providing "decent support") which can be construed by courts as "civilly significant acts, which identify the priest as the diocese's 'agent.'"[35] Even though they have no canonical effect whatsoever, the priest's accepted resignation and the bishop's or major superior's notification of termination have been recognized by some courts as severing any agency relationship between the priest and his diocese or religious institute and, therefore, absolving the latter of any liability for the priest's torts. The diocese or religious institute can still fulfill its obligation to see to the decent support of the cleric by labeling this support a "severance package."

This strategy of resignation or termination from the priesthood is a clever piece of legal legerdemain, but it appears to me to be a bit too clever. Since the notion of resigning or being terminated from the priesthood is a canonical and, more importantly, theological absurdity, documents of resignation or termination are canonically meaningless. They in no way alter the canonical relationship between a cleric and the diocese or religious institute in which he is incardinated or the mutual obligations between the two. It is far from certain that, when apprised that these documents have no meaning within the Church, courts will be willing to view them as anything more than a semantic subterfuge. Moreover, providing for a resigned or terminated cleric's "decent support" under the rubric of "severance pay" still necessitates the kind of ongoing contacts between a resigned or terminated cleric and his diocese or religious institute that some erroneously believe the Washington court in the Compcare case saw as evidence of an agency relationship.

Although canonical concepts do not always correspond exactly with those of American law (e.g., unlike most American courts, canon law never characterizes the priest-bishop relationship as an employment relationship), it seems a bit disingenuous to treat them as if the two exist in

---

[34] John A. Alesandro and Alan J. Placa, "Church Agents and Employees: Legal and Canonical Issues," *CLSA Proceedings* 58 (1996) 35-82.

[35] Ibid., 51.

different universes. A more honest approach would be to attempt to explain the relationship between an incardinated cleric and his bishop or major superior in the secular legal categories that most closely approximate the canonical and argue more persuasively than we have hitherto that neither ordination nor incardination alone creates an agency relationship between a cleric and the Church.

This approach has been reasonably successful in the area of temporal goods. Since American law does not recognize the canonical juridic personality of dioceses and parishes, church authorities fulfill their obligation to "take care that the ownership of ecclesiastical goods is safeguarded through civilly valid methods" (c. 1287, §1, 2) by civil incorporation or other devices available in their jurisdictions. In 1911, the Sacred Congregation of the Council ordered the bishops of the United States to choose the corporate model that most closely approximated the canonical.[36] Some dioceses retained and others later adopted the corporation sole model, in which all the assets of the diocese, parishes and their institutional apostolates are held by a corporation whose sole member is the diocesan bishop.[37] In theory, all assets of the corporation sole, both those belonging to the juridic person of the diocese and those belonging to the juridic persons of its parishes, could be attached to satisfy tort judgments against a diocese for sexual abuse of minors by clerics. Nevertheless, at least in some places,[38] the Church has been successful in convincing courts that, despite a diocese's civil status as corporation sole, parish property was held by the corporation in trust for local congregations and was not, therefore, subject to attachment for payment of diocesan obligations.[39] If the Church can convince American courts to interpret the law governing corporation sole in a way that reflects canonical notions of the ownership of church property, it should not be impossible to convince the same courts that ordination and incardination alone do not make priests "agents" of the Church.

---

[36] Sacred Congregation of the Council, letter, July 29, 1911: *CLD* 2: 443-445.

[37] Paul G. Kauper and Stephen C. Ellis, "Religious Corporations and the Law," *University of Michigan Law Review* 71 (1973) 1540-1541.

[38] One of these places is the State of Montana. For this information, I am indebted to Dr. James Provost, former Chancellor of the Diocese of Helena, Montana, and current Professor of Canon Law at the Catholic University of America.

[39] See Brendan F. Brown, *The Canonical Juristic Personality with Special Reference to its Status in the United States of America*, Canon Law Studies 139 (Washington: Catholic University, 1927) 148. For a similar finding in a case where the property was held by the Archbishop in fee simple, see Mannix v. Purcell, 46 Ohio St. 102, 24 N.E. 595 (1988) and Kauper and Ellis, 1523.

Proponents of resignation or termination as a strategy for distancing dioceses and religious institutes from sexually abusive clerics overlook the fact that it is not the existence of an agency relationship alone that can lead to the Church being held negligently liable for priests' torts. To find an institution liable for negligent supervision, the court must find in addition that it was "on notice" about its agent's potential for aberrant behavior and that, once "on notice," it failed to do what a reasonable person would do to prevent such misconduct. In the end, it is less important to eradicate every trace of an agency relationship between the Church and a priest with a record of sexual misconduct than to be able to convince the court that the Church did all it could be reasonably expected to do to prevent further misconduct.

2. Modifications in the Judicial Penal Process

For those worried about potential liability for the torts of unassigned and unassignable clerics and uncertain that documents of resignation or termination offer sufficient protection, the only canonical method for severing the relationship between a cleric and the Church has, until recently, been the imposition of the penalty of dismissal from the clerical state through the judicial penal process. Several obstacles stand in the way of the use of this process. First, the process itself is complex, cumbersome and time-consuming and few tribunals in the United States, whose almost exclusive mission has been the expeditious processing of marriage nullity cases, have experience in using it. Second, canon 1395, §2 of the revised code provides for the penalty of dismissal from the clerical state for clerics guilty of sins against the Sixth Commandment of the Decalogue with minors "below the age of sixteen," but not for such sins with older minors. However, many, perhaps the majority, of the victims of clergy sexual abuse in the United States have been sixteen or seventeen years old when the abuse occurred.[40] Thus, the canonical penal process is not available for dealing with these cases. Although particular law can provide penalties for sexual offenses not included in canon 1395, particular law cannot threaten the penalty of dismissal from the clerical state (c. 1317). Third, many of the accusations of sexual abuse brought against clerics involve events that took place many years in the past. However, the penal action for prosecuting offenses mentioned in canon 1395 is extinguished by prescription when five years

---

[40] Jenkins, 78-80; Rossetti, *A Tragic Grace*, 88.

have elapsed since the date of the delict (c. 1362, §1, 2-§2). Consequently, no penal action is available for prosecuting many cases.

In an effort to remove these obstacles to the use of the penal process, the National Conference of Catholic Bishops of the United States entered into discussions with the Holy See about possible derogations from universal law. An interdicasterial committee composed of representatives of the Congregation for Clergy, the Congregation for Sacraments and Divine Worship and the Apostolic Signatura was formed to discuss these issues with the representatives of the American bishops.[41] To rid the penal process of some of its complexity and clumsiness, the bishops proposed an administrative procedure modeled on the procedure for the removal of pastors (cc. 1740-1747) that would allow diocesan bishops to impose the penalty of dismissal from the clerical state without a trial. Dismissed clerics would have had the right to make recourse to the Apostolic See against bishops' decrees of dismissal. The interdicasterial committee rejected this proposed administrative procedure as insufficiently sensitive to the rights of clerics.

The American bishops were more successful, however, in securing for the United States modifications of the provisions of universal law on the scope of the delict of sexual abuse of minors by clerics and the period of prescription for the penal action for prosecuting it. On April 25, 1994, the Holy Father issued a rescript in response to the petition of the President of the NCCB, which granted "certain derogations... from the canons of the Code of Canon Law about the penal process pertaining to a delict against the Sixth Commandment of the Decalogue committed by a cleric with a minor."[42] First, the delict punishable with the penalty of dismissal from the clerical state of canon 1395, §2 is extended to include sins against the Sixth Commandment with any minor.[43] Second, the period of prescription for the penal action for this delict is extended to ten years, and it is now to be computed not from the day on which the delict was perpetrated (c. 1362, §2) but from the date of the victim's eighteenth birthday.[44] Moreover, as long as the victim had made a denunciation of the delict prior to his or her twenty-eighth birthday, the

---

[41] National Conference of Catholic Bishops, *Canonical Delicts Involving Sexual Misconduct and Dismissal from the Clerical State* (Washington: United States Catholic Conference, 1995) 1.

[42] John Paul II, "Rescript from and Audience with His Holiness," April 25, 1994, in John A. Alesandro, "Dismissal from the Clerical State in Cases of Sexual Misconduct: Recent Derogations," *CLSA Proceedings* 56 (1994) 63.

[43] Ibid.

[44] Ibid.

period of prescription is extended by one year from the date of the denunciation.[45]

Since these derogations have only prospective effect, they apply only to delicts committed after April 24, 1994. Nevertheless, the rescript also alters the period of prescription for delicts committed prior to this date. Although the period itself remains five years as in canon 1362, §1, 2, it now runs not from the date of the offense, but from the date of the victim's eighteenth birthday.[46] This last derogation is itself a notable departure from the basic principle of penal law that "if a law is changed after an offense has been committed the law which is more favorable to the accused is to be applied (c. 1313, §1)."

These derogations were intended to facilitate the use of the canonical penal process for imposing penalties on clerics who had sexually abused minors. Nevertheless, since 1994, there has been no noteworthy increase in the number of penal cases introduced into ecclesiastical tribunals in the United States. The most commonly cited reason for the dearth of penal cases in American tribunals remains that its procedural complexity renders it difficult to utilize. It is unlikely, however, that American tribunals will develop greater proficiency in applying the norms for the judicial penal process in the foreseeable future since the Apostolic See has recently introduced a much simpler administrative procedure for the dismissal of delinquent clerics.

3. An Administrative Procedure for Dismissal

The first signs of this new procedure appeared in June of 1998 when the news media reported that three priests, two in Boston and one in Dallas, who had admitted to sexual abuse of minors, had been penally dismissed from the clerical state by the Roman Pontiff personally. The one rescript I have been able to review reads:

The Supreme Pontiff John Paul II, after having heard the report of the Most Eminent Cardinal Secretary of State concerning the delicts mentioned in can. 1395, §2 perpetrated by the aforementioned presbyter of the diocese of D. in the United States of America, after having examined the impossibility of proceeding to this dismissal from the clerical state through the judicial penal process according to the norms of cann. 1342, §2 and 1425, §1, 2, a), after those preliminary formalities mentioned in

---

[45] Ibid.
[46] Ibid.

cann. 1717-1719 have been completed, by a decision that is supreme and unappealable and liable to no recourse, decrees that the previously mentioned penalty of dismissal is to be imposed on the said priest.

The decree is printed on the letterhead of the Congregation for Divine Worship and the Discipline of the Sacraments. To it are appended the usual conditions and restrictions imposed by the Congregation in rescripts of "laicization" (with the addition of the word "dismissal" at several points) and the signatures of the Congregation's prefect and sub-secretary.

News reports about these dismissals raised eyebrows in canonical circles because the Holy See had previously resisted requests for administrative dismissals of clerics because of its concerns about honoring the rights of the accused. The case cited here raised precisely these concerns since the dismissal was announced to the press not only before it was communicated to the dismissed priest, who was then serving a life term in a state prison for his crimes, but before he was even aware that a procedure for his dismissal was underway. Although Pope John Paul II has insisted that the "right of defense" is required by the natural law itself,[47] it is hard to see how the "right of defense" was honored in this dismissal case.

Perhaps out of sensitivity to the "right of defense," the Roman Curia has developed an informal, but, to my knowledge at least, unpublished procedure for the administrative dismissal of priests. The basic requirements of this process were summarized in a private letter to a diocesan bishop from the Congregation of the Clergy:

1. the diocesan bishop where the cleric to be dismissed is incardinated must request the use of this procedure *ex officio* and *in poenam* in a letter in which he explains the reason why it is impossible to use the judicial penal process;

2. the diocesan bishop is to include a letter in which he renews his request to the cleric to petition the Holy Father personally for a return to the lay state through a dispensation from the obligations of the clerical state and in which he reminds the cleric that there is more dignity in making such a request than in being dismissed from the clerical state as a penalty;

3. if the cleric refuses this encouragement to request a return to the lay state, his letter of refusal, which can be prepared with the assistance

---

[47] John Paul II, "Allocutio ad Romanae Rotae auditores, officiales et advocatos coram admissos," January 26, 1989: *AAS* 81 (1989) 922-927.

of an advocate, should contain his reasons for this refusal and his defense of himself and his actions that have prompted the request for his dismissal from the clerical state; and

4. the dossier should include:
   a) a copy of the sentence(s) of conviction by the secular tribunal(s);
   b) a document attesting the ordination of the priest in question; and
   c) the votum of the promotor of justice of the diocesan tribunal.

Although it is not known how frequently this procedure has been invoked, it raises many questions, some of them troubling. Is it available only for punishing the delict of sexual abuse of minors or can it be requested for other, less severe delicts? Can the procedure be requested only when the priests has been convicted in criminal court or is it also available when there has been a civil judgment assessing tort liability, when a civil suit was initiated but settled out of court, or even when there has been no involvement of the secular courts? Can the procedure be applied when the impossibility of initiating a judicial penal process results from extinction of the penal action by the operation of prescription?

It is also not clear what evidentiary standard has to be met in order for the penalty of dismissal to be inflicted. In the canonical judicial process, judges cannot issue a condemnatory sentence unless they have reached moral certainty about the defendant's commission of the delict and imputability (c. 1608, §1). Moral certainty is characterized by "the exclusion of well-founded or reasonable doubt."[48] However, in civil cases, American courts generally require that plaintiffs prove their case only by the preponderance of evidence rather than by the more stringent standard of "guilt beyond a reasonable doubt" which is required in criminal cases. Even in criminal trials, accused priests, while maintaining their innocence, have sometimes pled guilty as part of a "plea bargain" to secure more lenient treatment from the courts. Moreover, in the climate of hysteria over child abuse in the United State during the past decade, there have been several highly publicized cases in which defendants were wrongly convicted and later exonerated.[49] If the procedure can be requested even when there has been no prior decision by a secular court, the Congregation's decision would have to be made on the basis of the diocese's own internal investigation, the results of which are

[48] Pius XII, "Allocutio ad Romanae Rotae auditores, officiales et advocatos coram admissos," October 1, 1942: AAS 34 (1942) 339.
[49] Jenkins, 83-90, 140-147.

not normally shared with the accused priest until a trial begins.[50] If a diocese finds itself incapable of initiating a judicial penal process, one can easily wonder about its capacity for a thorough investigation of a complaint.

By requiring that the priest whose dismissal is being requested be given the opportunity to defend himself and his actions and allowing him the assistance of an advocate to do so, the Congregation's procedure makes a modest provision for him to exercise the "right of defense." It is, however, only a modest provision. It does not guarantee the priest the right to review the evidence on the basis of which the decision will be made, to submit additional exculpatory evidence, to know and rebut the arguments proposed in favor of dismissal, to be represented by an advocate before the Congregation, or many of the other procedural protections generally associated with the "right of defense."[51] It is disturbing that a procedure for imposing the severe penalty of dismissal from the clerical state provides such minimal procedural protection for those who must bear its brunt.

4. Does American Law Necessitate Administrative Dismissal?

This relatively simple administrative procedure now available for dismissal is the result of the often hysterical fear that the Church in the United States would be bankrupted by astronomical liability judgments for negligence unless a way was found to dismiss clerics who had abused minors from the clerical state. That fear, grounded in an erroneous reading of the decision in the Doe v. Compcare case, has had a paralyzing effect on the ability of church leaders to imagine alternatives to distancing and dismissal for dealing with priests who have abused minors. There are, no doubt, some priest offenders who are so recalcitrant that they cannot responsibly be returned to ministry and probably should be dismissed. However, many others, after extensive therapy, have excellent prognoses for return to some form of ministry without serious risk of further abuse.[52] Of course, no amount of therapy can

---

[50] See Michaele Lega and Victorio Bartocetti, *Commentarium in iudicia ecclesiastica iuxta Codicem Iuris Canonici* (Rome: Anonima Libreria Cattolica Italiana, 1950) 3: 320.

[51] See Grzegorz Erlebach, *La nullità della sentenza giudiziale "ob ius defensionis denegatum" nella giurisprudenza rotale*, Studi Giuridici 25 (Vatican City: Libreria Editrice Vaticana, 1991) and Ann Jacobs, *Le droit de la défense dans les procès en nullité de mariage: étude de la jurisprudence rotale* (Paris: Éditions du Cerf, 1998).

[52] Rossetti, *A Tragic Grace*, 88-96.

guarantee that a person will never offend again and recidivism after a priest has been returned to ministry will almost certainly prompt a multi-million dollar law suit.

The outcome of such a law suit will hinge not on whether the recidivist was an "agent" of the diocese or religious institute or whether the Church was "on notice" about his proclivities but on whether the Church did what a reasonable person would do to prevent the priest's from offending. Of course, one young person molested by a priest is one too many. Nevertheless, no approach to dealing with abusive clerics can guarantee that they will never offend again. The critical criterion for the "reasonableness" of approaches to dealing with clerics who have abused minors in the past is really which available approach is most likely to protect minors from sexual abuse in the future.

Dismissing priest abusers from the clerical state or refusing them assignments in ministry and allowing them to exist in a sort of limbo on the margins of the Church may distance the Church sufficiently from these clerics to allow the Church to escape liability for negligence if they offend again. However, these strategies leave these priests in society without supervision, continued treatment and restrictions on their contacts with minors. In addition, these marginalized clerics or former clerics are likely to be under a high degree of stress, to be isolated from peers and without a social support network, and to be overwhelmed by feelings of loneliness, emptiness and despair. These are precisely the circumstances which, clinicians note, are high risk factors for recidivism.[53]

On the other hand, reassigning a cleric who has responded well to treatment and received a favorable prognosis to a supervised ministry with strict limits on his contacts with minors provides him with regular contacts with peers, a familiar social and spiritual support network, and an opportunity to contribute in a meaningful way, albeit more limited than he might like, to the mission of the Church to which he has dedicated his life and which has not now abandoned him in his darkest hour. Even the most favorable circumstances cannot guarantee against another fall from grace, and the political climate in the Church in the United States may not yet be ready for the second approach.[54] However, all things considered, which approach is a more reasonable way of protecting vulnerable young people? When cases of clerical sexual abuse of

---

[53] Lothstein, 108-109.

[54] For a strong and sometimes strident argument against this second approach, see Nicholas P. Cafardi, "Stones Instead of Bread: Sexually Abusive Priests in Ministry," *Studia canonica* 27 (1993) 145-172.

minors come before American courts, the key question is not whether the Church succeeded in preventing such abuse, but whether the Church did what a reasonable person would do to prevent it.

IV. CONCLUSION

The revelation that priests in the United States have sexually abused young people has prompted a thorough reassessment of the ways in which the Church screens candidates for ordained ministry and deals with accusations of misconduct. The policies and procedures that resulted from this reassessment have been, in the main, salutary and consistent with the norms of canon law. However, the criticism directed at the Church by victims of clergy abuse and others, including at times the media, for its supposed slowness to recognize the problem of clergy sexual abuse and its perceived ineptness in dealing with it has led to a felt need on the part of some church authorities to be – and, perhaps more importantly, to be perceived as – "tough on" sexual predators within the clergy.

This desire to "get tough" was certainly prompted by the desire to prevent the sexual abuse of young people. However, fear of astronomical civil judgments for negligent supervision has also been a driving force behind some of these policies and practices. Requirements of psychological testing and other types of invasive background checks which are violative of the right to privacy are designed, in part, to provide a "paper trail" so that, in the event of a law suit, the Church can document that it had done everything possible to screen its ministers and candidates for ministry. The swift and simple procedure for the administrative dismissal from the clerical state was urgently sought, in large part, because of the fear that secular courts would hold dioceses and religious institutes liable for negligent supervision if a priest, known by church authorities to have been involved in sexual abuse in the past, should offend again while still a cleric.

Both of these canonically questionable approaches to the problem of clergy sexual abuse are based on flawed readings of the applicable American law. Courts have not required the Church to do "everything possible" to screen out unfit ministers and candidates for ministry but to do what a "reasonable" person would do to insure ministerial fitness. Moreover, the courts have been respectful of the limits imposed on the Church's ability to screen ministers and candidates by the right of privacy, recognized in both canon and secular laws.

Nor have secular courts moved to hold church institutions negligent in supervising clerics simply because they were still incardinated in dioceses or religious institutes at the time of their offenses. The much cited but misunderstood holding of the Washington State appellate court decision in the Compcare case was that the diocese's involvement with a priest while he was living in Washington state was sufficient to give a Washington court jurisdiction to examine the issue of whether these contacts amounted to negligent supervision. While the court found that, when viewed in the light most favorable to plaintiffs, there was sufficient *prima facie* evidence to support a cause of action against the diocese, it rather pointedly refused to rule on the issue of negligence. To derive from this isolated case a general rule of law that the Church will be held liable for negligent supervision whenever an incardinated cleric with a past history of sexual abuse offends anew is contrary to what the decision expressly says and stretches its holding much farther than the case will bear.

Although both secular and ecclesiastical pundits often berate the litigious spirit that pervades American culture, this propensity to take disputes to the courts can also be seen as a recognition that with freedom comes responsibility. The constitutional system of the United States gives the Church broad freedom to conduct its mission in accord with its own canonical norms, but this system does not exempt the Church from the obligation of exercising this freedom in a responsible way. Secular law does not require that the Church remove every stain of sin from the body ecclesiastic but that it exercise a reasonable standard of care in choosing and assigning ordained ministers. No amount of care by the Church will spare it the trial – and embarrassment – of law suits. But reasonable and responsible action will allow the Church to prevail in the suits that will inevitably come.

This brief survey of the Church's response to the problem of clergy sexual abuse in the United States and the role secular law – or, more precisely, misperceptions of secular law – has played in shaping this response underscores the fact that the Church lives and moves and has its being at the crossroads of two laws, one canonical and the other secular. Those who serve the Church as lawyers need to be knowledgeable about and attentive to both laws. Ignorance of or inattention to secular law can leave the Church not only exposed to the risk of liability for damages but liable to take hasty, unnecessary and ultimately counterproductive actions. Ignorance of or inattention to canon law can lead to a style of governance that implicitly treats the Church more as a secular

corporation than as the pilgrim people of God and compromises the theological values enshrined in the Church's law. Knowledge of and attentiveness to both canon and secular law characterized the life and work of
Monsignor Onclin, to whose memory this lecture is dedicated. May we
on both sides of the Atlantic who continue his work honor his legacy by
placing our knowledge of and attentiveness to both laws at the service of
the Church.

UNITY AMONG THE ORTHODOX CHURCHES. FROM THE THEOLOGICAL APPROACH TO THE HISTORICAL REALITIES

CHARALAMBOS K. PAPASTATHIS

Chronologically, the first core of the Church was the parish. The Apostles founded Christian communities, where followers gathered around the common altar. The formation of the clergy took place gradually. In chronological order, first came the higher clergy, which included -as it does today-, the deacons, the presbyters and the bishops. This process of formation was completed by the first half of the second century. These persons were ordained by the Apostles, later by their successors and finally by the bishops. This is how the principle of "apostolic succession" came into being and, at the same time, the unity of the Church, based on two foundations: holy communion and the bishop.

After the reordering of the state organization by Diocletian, there was a tendency for the unification of a number of bishops into broad administrative units. The center of these units was the mother-city of the larger province. They were named metropolises, and the bishop of the mother-city was called a metropolitan. He had seniority in honor and authority over the bishops, who were the heads of the dioceses of his metropolis. After the Second Ecumenical Council in 381, there were frictions among metropolises over the acquisition of super-metropolitan authority. In this conflict, the seats of Rome, Constantinople, Alexandria and Antioch prevailed. The Third Ecumenical Council in 431 added the seat of Jerusalem. These five metropolises were termed patriarchates, and the entire Roman empire was distributed among them. This system was called "the pentarchy of the patriarchs". Only one exception was allowed (which remains in force): the island of Cyprus became an autocephalous Church following a decision of the Third Ecumenical Council. This system of administration of the Church was in effect for centuries. During this period, in certain regions, changes in the ecclesiastical structure took place, but they were short-lived. Until the great schism in 1054, the structure of the Church remained basically as it had been shaped during the fifth century.

In the year 330, Constantine the Great moved the seat of the empire to Constantinople, the New Rome. This constituted an event of tremendous significance, whose consequences persist to this day. The bishop of Constantinople, despite the elevation of his see to second in rank as concerns seniority in honor (after the bishop of Rome), and despite its characterization as Ecumenical, was always second in the capital, after the emperor. This situation was reinforced by the framework of relations between State and Church in the Roman empire, caesaropapism. By contrast in the West, the bishop of Rome remained first in everything. He was the center of religious and political life and consequently of cultural life as well. A different system of relations between Church and the various states of Western and Central Europe prevailed there, hierocracy.

At the same time the patriarchal pentarchy came into being, the institution of autocephaly made its appearance. This Greek term signifies a Church that has its own head, whose leader (the "first") is elected without interference from any other Church. In other words, it is an independent Church, as the five patriarchates were. At several times and for various reasons (even political ones, although always cloaked in religious covering), some regions of the West and the East acquired the autocephalous regime and more sought to acquire it. But only temporarily. However, in Eastern and Southeastern Europe, the mimicking of the culture and structures of the Roman empire by the leaders of new states, led them to request that the Mother-Church of Constantinople grant an autocephalous regime to the Church of their own province. They considered it a necessary supplement to their state's independence and their sovereign's prestige. This is because, in the East, the principle of state supremacy prevailed, while in the West, that of Church supremacy was prevalant, always with the anticipated fluctuations.

The coexistence of the five patriarchates and the autocephalous Churches, each one with its specific region, did not contradict the spiritual structure of the One, Holy, Catholic and Apostolic Church. Let us take ecclesiastical "citizenship" as an example. When a Christian from Smyrna, which fell within the region of Constantinople, was situated in Marseilles, he received the sacraments from the Western Church, and the inverse was also true. Ecclesiastical "citizenship" was determined by locus, not origin. However, after the schism, this unity was breached. It was preserved in the regions of the four patriarchates and the Church of Cyprus in the East, but not between these Churches and Rome.

The unity that exists among the Orthodox Churches is not different from that of the first centuries. It is distinguished by dogmatic unity and by canonical or organic unity. The first is expressed by the unfaltering observance of the doctrines and the holy tradition, as they were preserved by the One, Holy, Catholic and Apostolic Church before the schism. The second manifests itself in a number of ways. The first of these is the observance of at least the basic holy canons and institutions of the first seven Ecumenical Councils and those of the local councils that were recognized as having ecumenical status. Basic holy canons and institutions are those that principally make known the Orthodox character of the Church, e.g. the synodal regime. The second of these ways is the identity of the organic system of the Church, whose main elements are the parish, the diocese and the synod. The third way is the preservation of very close ties between the local Churches. These ties are expressed by the communication they maintain and by their participation in events of great importance, as well as by the mention of their "heads" in the diptychs during mass. Finally, there is the existence of a common agency, which is the focus of the congruous volition of the Orthodox totality, when such volition exists. In this respect, the Orthodox Churches appear to be what would best be described as a federation with a precedence of honor (not authority) given to the Ecumenical Patriarchate, a fact which is acknowledged by all the Orthodox Churches. This precedence is the source of the duty and the mission of the Ecumenical Patriarchate to take initiative and undertake pan-orthodox efforts to regulate problems which arise either in relations between the Churches or within a single Church, as was the case two years ago with the convocation of a pan-orthodox meeting in Sofia concerning the elimination of internal controversies in the Church of Bulgaria.

Nevertheless, this precedence of Constantinople has been long disputed, specifically since the fifteenth century. Then, the most significant events in the East (which occurred contemporaneously) were the fall of the Roman empire and the resurrection of Russia. The former was subjugated under the Asiatic Ottoman yoke; the latter was freed from the Asiatic Tatar yoke. This coincidence contributed to the formulation of the theory about Moscow as the Third Rome. The union of the two great Churches, that had been accomplished during the Ferrara-Florence Council, had fundamentally diminished the prestige of the Church of Constantinople in the conscience of the Russian people. The charm of the Roman empire as the gatekeeper of the Orthodox traditions slackened. The Fall of Constantinople that took place a few years after the Union (1453) was seen by the Russians as divine punishment for the betrayal of Orthodox faith. But, if the first and the second Rome had been lost, the Orthodox reign had not come to an end, and would never be lost. God may have allowed the faithless to subjugate the Greeks, but He would never allow the annihilation of the Orthodox doctrine and the triumph of the Latin and the Muslims over it. According to the discourse which had developed in Russia, the old, first Rome had been lost, since it fell into the heresy of the *azyma* (the unleavened), and the second, Constantinople, because it acceded to the heresy of the former. Moscow is the Third Rome. And, adds the Russian messianism, there will be no fourth Rome.

The theory of the Third Rome did not concern only the Church of Constantinople, but the entire Roman empire. The Third Rome did not merely succeed it. It replaced it. Thus, the ruler of Moscow became the Tsar (emperor), the metropolitan of Moscow became the ecumenical agent of the true faith and the Russian state incorporated all Christian kingdoms. To support these views, mythological traditions were devised, such as the founding of the Church of Russia by the Apostle Andrew, also founder of the Church of Constantinople according to the tradition. Consequently, the Church of Russia was also apostolic and had to rid itself from the patronage of Constantinople.

The theory of the Third Rome was disputed by the adherents of panslavism. George Križanić, a Catholic priest from Croatia and a graduate of the Pontifical Greek College of Rome, conceived the theory of panslavism during his exile at Tobol'sk of Siberia (1663-1665). Under this theory, Divine Providence calls on Moscow to become the head not only of the Orthodox, but of the entire Slavic world, concentrating under its leadership all Slavic peoples regardless of religious doctrine. This theory was pioneering, not only for Russia, considering that the Thirty Years' War had just ended, having divided the Catholics and the Protestants of Western and Central Europe. Undoubtedly, the hardest blow to the theory of the Third Rome was delivered by the turn of Peter the Great towards the West and his struggle for the europeanization of Russia. Nevertheless, the vision of the Third Rome does not cease to inspire the Russian Church, even to this day. Whenever possible, the Russian Church sought to impose itself over the other Orthodox Churches. During the 19th and in the beginning of the 20th century, flocks of Russian monks settled in Palestine and Mount Athos. Thanks to the generous economic assistance of St. Petersburg, they managed to substantially alter the ethnological composition of monasticism in these two regions. They would have prevailed completely, if the Revolution of 1917 had not occurred. In addition to the latter, especially in Mount Athos, the heresy of the Imjabožiki (the Worshippers of the Divine Name) spread among the Russian monks, then was propagated to Russia itself. In 1914, after receiving permission from the Greek Government, Russian war ships anchored in the harbor of Daphni, and Russian military forces landed at the holy peninsula, arresting hundreds of Russian Imjabožiki, who were taken to Odessa.

In the years following the schism, important changes occurred in the structure of the Eastern Church. The patriarchates of Alexandria, Antioch and Jerusalem, which had for centuries dwindled because of the occupation of their provinces by the Arab Muslims, were subjected to a further deterioration of their already critical condition because of the Crusades. The crusaders founded new Churches of Western dogmatic and administrative structure on the territories they occupied. The West did not seek simply to push Islam out of the Eastern Mediterranean, but also to take its place. On their route towards the Holy Land in 1204, the empire offered hospitality in Constantinople to the men of the fourth crusade. In violation of the rules of hospitality, they seized it, raided the place and split the territories of the empire among themselves. They appointed their own Latin patriarch in Constantinople. They plundered and pillaged the monuments and the holy relics that are currently on display in museums and in churches of Western and Central Europe. Although within a few decades the empire managed to retrieve its capital, it was already too weak to be able to face the onslaught of the Ottoman invasion. Despite the 800 years that have since passed, the fall of the city of cities to the Christians of the West is permanently kept alive in the memories of the Greeks. This sentiment of bitterness was the most effective factor for the reinforcement of the anti-unionist faction and, at present, helps foster the anti-ecumenical one.

Since the time of its creation, the Christian Roman empire had supported the One, Holy, Catholic and Apostolic Church by granting privileges. It used the Orthodox doctrine to bind together the numerous nations and races across its vast territory. Through the work of its zealous missionaries, it propagated Christianity and the Letters to the peoples that lived around its borders. I will limit myself to the mention of Ulfila among the Goths and the brothers Constantine-Cyril and Methodius among the Slavs. The acceptance of Christianity by these peoples marked their entry into the civilized world. Further, it signified the mimicking of the imperial model in state, religious and personal life. It was expected that newly-formed states, such as Bulgaria, Serbia, and later Russia, request an autocephalous ecclesiastical regime for their provinces, as a necessary complement for their state entity and for the prestige of their ruler. In practice, the demand for the acquisition of autocephaly was almost always an act of state policy. It is not without significance that the Ecumenical Councils did not deal with the canonical preconditions for the granting of autocephaly. The relevant preconditions developed in practice, not by holy canons. Four prerequisites had to occur cumulatively. First, a need of ecclesiastical character was necessary. The usual prerequisite invoked is the creation of a state. The independence of the local Church is considered a necessary supplement to its own dominion. A relevant mention is made in the opinion of Patriarch Photios: "According to usage, the ecclesiastical regions, especially the jurisdictions upon the parishes, change at the same time that the state territories and administrations change."[1] Regardless of the intent of Photios when uttering this phrase, the fact is that he pointed out that the concurrent change is usual; hence, it is not a necessary requirement. From the aspect of ecclesiastical practice, the creation of a state can become the cause for the granting of autocephaly only if the need of the local Church is invoked, e.g. if there are difficulties in communication with the ecclesiastical center. Second, there must be a statement by the whole body of the congregation (laymen and clergy) that it wishes the elevation of its Church to autocephalous status. Third, the granting of autocephaly must be by the Mother-Church under whose spiritual and administrative jurisdiction the provinces seeking autocephaly belong. Finally, the relevant act ("Tomos") of the Mother-Church must be acknowledged by the other Orthodox Churches, that in this regard function within the limits set by the act itself. The same holds for the further unification of other regions with a Church that is already autocephalous. Autocephaly should be distinguished from autonomy and semi-autonomy as structures of a Church. These are also regimes of self-administration, but they maintain a degree of dependence upon the Mother Church, usually in the form of the approval of the election of their new "head".

As a political goal of the state, autocephaly almost always causes conflict between the Mother-Church and the interested party. These conflicts caused disruption in the overall unity among the Orthodox Churches. Today, in addition to the four ancient Patriarchates and the Archdiocese of Cyprus, nine other Churches are autocephalous, most of which were detached from the Ecumenical Patriarchate. They are the

---

[1] In his letter (of the year 861) addressed to the Pope of Rome Nicholas I; see B. LAOURDAS-L.G. WESTERINK, *Photii Patriarchae Constantinopolitani epistulae et amphilochia*, vol. III, Leipzig 1985, p. 136.

Churches of Russia (1448; 1452), Greece (1833; 1850), Serbia (1879), Romania (1867; 1885), Poland (1924), Albania (1922, 1929; 1937), Bulgaria (1870; 1945), Georgia (1927; 1991), and Czechia and Slovakia (1998). The Orthodox Church of Finland is autonomous. The first of the abovementioned dates refers to the year in which autocephaly was unofficially proclaimed, and the second to the year of the official acknowledgment. In almost all cases, problematic situations occurred. When the metropolitan of Russia, Isidoros, returned to his seat in 1441 after the Council of Ferrara-Florence and wished to impose the union of the Churches there, the ruler of Moscow ordered his arrest and indictment. The ecclesiastical court was composed exclusively of Russian prelates. Consequently, in 1448, these same prelates elected a new metropolitan of Russia. It was the first time that the metropolitan of Russia was not tried and elected respectively by the Synod of the Ecumenical Patriarchate, under whose region the Church of Russia belonged. Thus, it became *de facto* independent. No doubt, there were strong reactions concerning the abovementioned actions within Russia. Finally, the ruler Vasilij Vasil'evič turned to the emperor Constantine Palaeologos for the settlement of the matter in 1452. During that same year, the Church of Russia became *de jure* autocephalous.

The autocephaly of the Church of Greece was a lot more painful. During the War of Independence that erupted in 1821, communication between the bishops of the insurgent provinces and the Ecumenical Patriarchate was not possible. After the liberation of Greece, there were several people who advocated the acquisition of autocephaly. This was accomplished in 1833. But it took place by coup, with the promulgation of a law on the part of the government, without observing the canonical requirements for its granting. This resulted in a disruption of the unity between the autocephalous -as it had been declared- Church on the one hand and the Ecumenical Patriarchate and the other Orthodox Churches on the other. The root of the problem centered around the manner of the acquisition of autocephaly. This isolation of the Church of the new kingdom was the reason that the Constitution of 1844 included a provision, according to which: "...the Orthodox Church of Greece, acknowledging our Lord Jesus Christ as its head, is inseparably united in doctrine with the Great Church of Christ in Constantinople and with every other Church of Christ of the same doctrine, observing unwaveringly, as they do, the holy apostolic and synodal canons and sacred traditions..." (article 2). This provision aimed at declaring the orthodoxy of the Church of Greece, despite the breach of its unity with the other Churches. This

unpleasant situation ended happily in 1850. The Mother-Church of Constantinople issued a "Tomos" whereby it granted the Church of Greece
an autocephalous regime *ex nunc*, that is, starting from 1850. However,
although the "Tomos" reinstated the Church in Greece to its normal status, the aforementioned provision was preserved in all subsequent Constitutions (1864, 1911, 1927, 1952, 1968), as well as in the current one
of 1975 (article 3, § 1). In fact, it gave the Church the possibility of
claiming that the Constitution recognizes the validity of all the holy
canons in general, as well as their prevalence over the formal laws of the
state. This constitutes another aspect of canonical unity, which is de
facto limited to the fundamental holy canons and institutions.

The Greek issue was settled over the course of seventeen years. The
respective Bulgarian situation took seventy-five years. Its particularity
lay in the fact that the autocephalous regime was sought for an Orthodox
people which lacked a state entity. The Bulgarians lived within the
Ottoman empire, together with other Orthodox nations. The election of
Bulgarian prelates for the Bulgarian provinces of Southeastern Europe,
as well as other arrangements, was the canonical solution, proposed by
the Mother-Church. However, Russian politics, that had never given up
on the legacy of Peter the Great for a descent towards the warm waters
of the Mediterranean, on the one hand and the Ottoman policy of *divide
et impera* on the other, led to the issuance of a sultanic firman that established an autocephalous Bulgarian Church (1870). Two years later, the
Synod of the Patriarchate of Constantinople, in which the patriarchs of
Alexandria and Antioch also participated, proclaimed this Church schis-
matic. The schism was lifted in 1945.

The pursuit of autocephaly by other Churches did not reach such
extreme situations, but it was not always uneventful. I believe that the
main reason behind the inducement of disputes lies in the fact that the
state was more interested in the acquisition of autocephaly than the official Church was. A characteristic case is the Church of Former Yugoslav
Republic of Macedonia. The Patriarchate of Serbia, as the Mother-
Church, had pronounced it autonomous in 1958. With the interference of
the authorities of the Federal Republic of Yugoslav-Macedonia, this
Church declared itself autocephalous in 1966. The Patriarchate of Serbia
did not recognize this coup and interrupted all relations with this
Church. All other Orthodox Churches did the same. This unpleasant situation continues to this day.

What is very often emphasized is the identification between a given
nation and its Orthodox Church. The latter considers itself "the national

Church". In this aphorism, autocephaly assumes primary significance, since the administration of the Church has its seat in the interior of the respective state. In this way, however, the defining characteristic of the local Orthodox Church ends up being extra-religious. Besides, the road to autocephaly has on several occasions brought about controversies of nationalistic character between various peoples. For example, the struggle of the Bulgarians to secure as many followers of their firman-founded Church (1870) as possible and to expand its region led them to warfare against other Orthodox nations and races in the wider area of Ottoman Macedonia and Thrace, as they resorted to proselytism, both religious and national. Later, during the first and second world wars, when Yugoslav Macedonia and Greek Macedonia and Thrace fell under Bulgarian rule, the occupying authorities persecuted the local clergymen and replaced them with others, brought in from Bulgaria.

Conflicts are not restricted only to wartime. We have recently witnessed the demands of the Church of Greece from its Mother-Church, the Ecumenical Patriarchate. It should be noted that the entire Greek territory does not constitute a uniform ecclesiastical region. The autocephalous Church is restricted to Southern Greece, whereas the northern regions of the country and the islands of the Eastern Aegean (the New Lands) continue to be spiritually subject to Constantinople. They are united with the autocephalous Church only administratively. The two of them together constitute the "Church of Greece", according to a law of the Greek state (1928) and a canonical act of the Patriarchate (1928). Furthermore, in Greece there is also the semi-autonomous Church of Crete (1900), the self-administrated Athos peninsula, whose bishop is the occasional Ecumenical Patriarch, and the Dodecanese, which is fully under the jurisdiction of the Patriarchate. Following the election of the new Archbishop of Athens in 1998, the Church of Greece appeared to be making claims against the Ecumenical Patriarchate. The first demand is grounded on the belief that the autocephaly of the Church of Greece is not full. The "Tomos" (1850) determines as its supreme authority only the Holy Synod and not the "first", its archbishop. This is in contrast with what happened with the "Tomoi" drafted for the other autocephalous Churches. Thus, the upgrading of autocephaly is sought. The second demand is that the archbishop of Athens is also mentioned in the New Lands, in parallel with the Patriarch. The mention of the name, however, denotes sovereign rights, which the autocephalous Church does not possess in the New Lands. Their administrative unification was executed by Constantinople by delegation, hence it is an authorization that may be revoked. Nevertheless, the newspaper reports that the auto-cephalous Church aspires to bring the entire Greek territory under its scepter, and even to expand towards the Diaspora. If these reports are accurate, the Church of Greece is not unique, to the extent that differen-tiations between the Orthodox Churches are not limited to the magnitude and the degree of autocephaly but are extended to the Diaspora as well.

We previously noted that ecclesiastical "citizenship" is determined by the place where the follower is located. Prior to the schism, a Christian who was located anywhere in the regions of the five Patriarchates or Cyprus was canonically subject to the local Church. What about the areas that lay beyond those regions? The view taught in the Greek-speaking Orthodox Churches constitutes a restrictive interpretation of the 28th canon of the Fourth Ecumenical Council that took place in Chal-cedon in 451. This canon, after confirming the equality of the preroga-tives of the Patriarchate of Constantinople to those of Rome, adds: "...Consequently, the metropolitans and they alone of the dioceses of Pontus, Asia and Thrace, as well as the bishops among the barbarians of the aforementioned dioceses, are to be ordained by the previously men-tioned very Holy See of the very Holy Church of Constantinople...".[2] Since bishops who belonged to the jurisdictions of Pontus, Asia and Thrace, and lived among the barbarians were thereafter ordained by Constantinople, it follows that "the barbarians" (those who were outside the regions of the empire) belonged to Constantinople. This issue became vital after the schism, when the Orthodox follower who was in the West, and the Roman Catholic who was in the East, could no longer have contact with the local Church. Thus, the Diaspora (Western, Cen-tral and Northern Europe, Asian territories beyond Pakistan and Afghanistan, and in recent years the American continent and Australia) came under the jurisdiction of the Ecumenical Patriarchate. But this has been recognized only by the Greek-speaking Orthodox Churches.

The disagreement of the other Churches is not so much due to the call-ing into question of the authenticity of the 28th canon of the Fourth Ecu-menical Council, by Slav Orthodox researchers, and not only by Roman Catholics. Instead it is due primarily to the desire of the Orthodox Churches to preserve close ethnic ties with their immigrants. For these people, the church is the center of their life in a foreign country: their hearth and altar. If their parish church does not belong to their own

---

[2] According to the translation of Archbishop PETER L' HUILLIER, *The Church of the Ancient Councils*, Crestwood, N.Y. 1996, p. 268.

national Church or if it does not cultivate their own cultural traditions and language, then there is the intense fear that the immigrants will be assimilated by their new environment and that they will be permanently lost for their country of origin. This does not interest only each particular Church, but also the relevant state. Thus, the various Churches have prelates, other clergymen and parishes in the Diaspora. A characteristic example is the great interest displayed by the communist governments of Eastern Europe in offering assistance to their local Church as concerns the Diaspora, whereas in the interior, they kept the Church in captivity. The Greek-speaking Churches (Alexandria, Jerusalem, Cyprus and Greece) generally respect and observe the interpretation handed down by the aforementioned canon regarding the jurisdiction of the Ecumenical Patriarchate. In addition to the Greeks, a number of Russian, Ukranian, Byelorussian, Latvian and Romanian immigrants in Western and Central Europe and America sought to come under the jurisdiction of the Patriarchate of Constantinople. They did not wish to be associated with the Churches of their fatherlands, because these had their seats in communist countries. They also did not want to be ministered by clergymen of their own nationality who lived abroad and did not maintain unity with the Orthodox Churches, due to fear of invalidity of the sacraments. In fact, an archdiocese, with its own hierarchy, parishes and language, has been set up expressly for the Russians and Ukrainians of Western Europe.

Indisputably, the coexistence of so many Orthodox Churches in the same territory disturbs unity among them. The founding of collective agencies, like the *Assemblée des Évêques Orthodoxes de France* in Paris or the *Standing Conference of Orthodox Bishops in America* (SCOBA) in 1960, constituted successful initiatives for the expansion of inter-orthodox cooperation. They became important fora in which bishops from various jurisdictions could meet regularly to discuss and act upon common issues which affected Orthodoxy in France and America. But, it is self-evident that they cannot be a substitute for unity itself, nor can they avert unpleasant incidents, such as the one that took place in the Moscow parishes in America. In 1970, the Patriarchate of Moscow, without consulting any other Orthodox Church, granted autocephaly to its independent metropolis in America. The title that was bestowed on it, the Orthodox Church of America, aimed at the assimilation of the Orthodox followers living there. Moreover, in 1973, the Patriarchate of Moscow accepted to grant autocephaly to the parishes that it had founded in Japan and in fact did so by underhand means. It submitted a proposal to the Central Committee of the World Council of Churches that the "autocephalous" Japanese Church be accepted in it, at a time when the latter had not officially become autocephalous. For the sake of historical accuracy, I should mention that the delegacy of the Church of Greece voted for the Russian proposal. Even among the Greek-speaking Churches, movements challenging the jurisdiction of the Ecumenical Patriarchate in the Diaspora have emerged. The aforementioned incident is not unique.

Personal differences led a deposed priest of the Orthodox Archdiocese of Australia, who directed a private Greek school in Melbourne, that was his own property, to bequeath it to the Holy Sepulcher as a metochion. A metochion is the accessory of a monastery, which is primarily of an economic character and purpose. The aforementioned transfer of property was not hindered by the laws of the state or the holy canons. But, those clergymen who came to Australia from Jerusalem did not stop at running the school. They also functioned as priests, independently from the local Archdiocese of the Ecumenical Patriarchate. With their actions, they divided the Greek Orthodox flock. The Ecumenical Patriarchate many times summoned them to revert to the way of the Church, but in vain. Finally, in 1993, it convoked a Mighty and Final Synod of the Greek-speaking Churches (Constantinople, Alexandria, Cyprus and Greece; Jerusalem, although it had been invited, refused to participate) in Istanbul, a Synod which tried and convicted the dissident clergymen of the Patriarchate of Jerusalem.

The Statutory Charter of the Church of Cyprus that is currently in force (1980) determines as its members not only the Orthodox inhabitants of the island, but also those who are natives of Cyprus and live abroad (article 2). Up until today, this statute has not yet come into effect, in the sense of the establishment of Cypriot parishes in the Diaspora. The subjugation of the Greeks of the Diaspora under a single Church does not only constitute a compliance with canonical tradition. It is at the same time a measure of protection of those legal relations that have a spiritual character, such as marriage. In Greece and in Cyprus, the alternative system is in effect concerning the celebration of marriage. Civil and religious marriage are equivalent. In fact, according to the older provisions of the Civil Code that were abrogated in Greece in 1982, only religious marriage was existent. But, in order for it to be valid, it had to be solemnized by a clergyman who retains his priesthood and belongs to an Orthodox Church that is in unity with the other Churches. As for the interior of Greece, there was no problem. But, in the Diaspora, there were cases where deposed clergymen or even non-ordained persons solemnized the sacrament of marriage. As a result, these marriages were later revealed to be non-existent under law, with tragic consequences concerning the legitimacy of children, inheritance and pension issues, etc. In Greek ecclesiastical law, the prevalent view is that the deposition of a cleric entails the forfeiture of priesthood, thus bringing about the non existence of the sacraments solemnized by him.

The conflicts that put unity to the test are not limited only to the occasional disputes of the seniority in honor of the Ecumenical Patriarchate, the disturbance of the peace in the Diaspora, or coups regarding the autocephalous regime. They extend to other areas as well, such as the calendar issue.

Despite the improvements featured by the Gregorian calendar in relation to the Julian one, the Orthodox Church disapproved of it. It believed that its implementation violated the provisions of the apostolic and synodal canons regarding the celebration of Easter. To look into the matter in greater detail, the Ecumenical Patriarchate convoked a Synod in 1593. The participants of this Synod were the Patriarchs of Constantinople, Alexandria, Antioch and Jerusalem (this one with a delegate) and forty-one bishops. The Synod decided not to adopt the Gregorian calendar, primarily because of the anomalies surrounding Easter. There was the possibility of having the celebration of Christian and Hebrew Easter on the same day, which was disallowed by the holy canons. In more recent years, there have been proposals for the introduction of the new calendar into the Church. The most significant action was the convocation of the Panorthodox Conference in the Ecumenical Patriarchate in 1921. The Conference, safeguarding the matter of Easter, did not concern itself with the introduction of the Gregorian calendar but with the amendment of the Julian calendar. This correction was not hindered from the aspect of holy canons. The Ecumenical Patriarchate proceeded with this correction, which it put into effect in 1924. In that same year, the Church of Greece did the same, but the other Churches did not. Since that time, however, some of them have come to accept the corrected calendar. Jerusalem, Russia, Serbia, and Mount Athos fully insist on the validity of the original Julian calendar. Regarding the celebration of Easter and any holidays that depend on it, there is no problem. Christmas, however, is celebrated by some Orthodox Churches on the 25th of December and by others on January 7. In addition to this differentiation between the Churches, the introduction of the amended Julian calendar created discord within the flock of the places where it was introduced. In Greece, a substantial number of followers did not accept this initiative. They set up their own altar, that of the Genuine Orthodox Christians. They have their own hierarchy, priests and parishes. They do not enjoy the privileges that the Greek state affords to the official Orthodox Church, as defined in article 3 of the Constitution. Parishes of the so-called Old-calendarists are also found in the Diaspora. They consider as non-existent the sacraments of all the Orthodox Churches, whether they have accepted or not the aforementioned corrected calendar, because the latter maintain unity with the former. Further, the Old-calendarists are in constant disagreement with the Ecumenical Patriarchate, because of the ecumenical contacts and the dialogue that it holds with the Catholic and the Protestant Churches. They charge that the Patriarchate has fallen into the "heresy of ecumenism". Among the various items included in the agenda of the Panorthodox Synod, whose convocation has been in prepartation for years, is the Diaspora, autocephaly and autonomy, the process of their proclamation, the common calendar, and the ecumenical movement.

If we leave out dogmatic unity, the canonical or organic unity of Orthodoxy is a rather relative concept. In this theological context there is no unity of administration comparable to the uniform administration of the Catholic Church. As a result, each particular Orthodox Church implements its own policy, giving the impression of a state organization. The incidents that I have mentioned are only indicative of the actual state of canonical unity, as experienced by the Church. After the downfall of the regimes of Eastern Europe and the territorial splintering-off that followed, one often hears wishes about Orthodox arrows, about the joint action of the Orthodox peoples and the like. Similarly, in the West, one hears comments about Orthodox fundamentalism. I think that reality is somewhat different. There is no common ground for the formation of alliances or the imposition of fundamentalism. The Orthodox Churches display a lack of accord on matters of ministry, much less can they establish a common course through the heated fields of world policy. Furthermore, there is another factor that obstructs the assumption of similar actions on their part: the state. Even in regions where the Orthodox comprise the overwhelming majority of the population and in places where the state displays a privileged interest in favor of the Orthodox Church, the Roman tradition of state supremacy has not ceased to be kept alive. No country has allowed the local Church to take initiatives of a non-religious character, much less to take actions related to the country's national defense or foreign policy. Anything that happens is attributable to individual initiatives taken by clergymen driven by fanaticism or personal ambition. It is indisputable that such actions lie beyond the framework of unity among the Orthodox Churches.

PERSONALIA

JOHN P. BEAL was born in Titusville, Pennsylvania in 1946. He studied theology at the University of Leuven (S.T.B., 1971; M.M.R.Sc., 1972) and canon law at the Catholic University of America (J.C.D., 1985). After eight years as judicial vicar of the Diocese of Erie (Pennsylvania), he was appointed to the faculty of the Department of Canon Law at the Catholic University of America, where he is associate professor and, since 1998, chair. J.P. Beal has published numerous articles and is co-editor of *A New Commentary on the Code of Canon Law* to be published by Paulist Press in 2000.

CHARALAMBOS K. PAPASTATHIS was born in Thessaloniki, Greece in 1940. He studied law at the Aristotle University of Thessaloniki (B.A. 1963). Post-graduate courses in the Vatican, Sofia, Bucharest and Prague. Assistant at the Center for Byzantine Studies (Aristotle University) in 1974. Ph. D. 1978. After three years of teaching Ecclesiastical Law at Democritus University (Komotini), he became "professeur agrégé" at the Faculty of Law (Aristotle University) in 1981 and full professor of Ecclesiastical Law in 1986. Secretary general of Cults at the Ministry of Education and Cults (1987-1988), president of the National Archives of Greece (1995-1997), member of the Administrative Committee of the National Library (1994-1999), vice-president of the Hellenic Association for Slavic Studies. He has published the following books: The legislative Work of the Cyrillo-Methodian Mission in Great Moravia; On the administrative Organization of the Church of Cyprus; The Charters of the Orthodox Communities of the Ottoman Empire; The Nomocanon of George Trapezountios; The Status of the Monks of Mount Athos; A Handbook of Ecclesiastical Law; Studies on the History of Thessaloniki and Macedonia; and more than 110 articles and reports in various reviews and symposia.

RIK TORFS was born in Turnhout, Belgium in 1956. He studied law at the University of Leuven (lic. iur., 1979; lic. not., 1980) and Canon Law at Strasbourg and Leuven University (J.C.D., 1987). After one year of teaching at Utrecht University (The Netherlands), he became professor at the Faculty of Canon Law (K.U. Leuven) in 1988. Dean of the Faculty of Canon Law since 1993 and visiting professor at the University of Stellenbosch (South Africa) since 2000, R. Torfs published seven books and more than 200 articles on canon law, law, church and state relationships. He is editor of the *European Journal for Church and State Research*.

PUBLICATIES / PUBLICATIONS
MSGR. W. ONCLIN CHAIR

Editor Rik Torfs

Canon Law and Marriage. Monsignor W. Onclin Chair 1995, **Leuven, Peeters, 1995, 36 p.**

R. TORFS, *The Faculty of Canon Law of K.U. Leuven in 1995*, 5-9.
C. BURKE, *Renewal, Personalism and Law*, 11-21.
R.G.W. HUYSMANS, *Enforcement and Deregulation in Canon Law*, 23-36.

A Swing of the Pendulum. Canon Law in Modern Society. Monsignor W. Onclin Chair 1996, **Leuven, Peeters, 1996, 64 p.**

R. TORFS, *Une messe est possible. Over de nabijheid van Kerk en geloof*, 7-11.
R. TORFS, *'Une messe est possible'. A Challenge for Canon Law*, 13-17.
J.M. SERRANO RUIZ, *Acerca del carácter personal del matrimonio: digresiones y retornos*, 19-31.
J.M. SERRANO RUIZ, *The Personal Character of Marriage. A Swing of the Pendulum*, 33-45.
F.G. MORRISEY, *Catholic Identity of Healthcare Institutions in a Time of Change*, 47-64.

In Diversitate Unitas. Monsignor W. Onclin Chair 1997, **Leuven, Peeters, 1997, 72 p.**

R. TORFS, *Pro Pontifice et Rege*, 7-13.
R. TORFS, *Pro Pontifice et Rege*, 15-22.
H. PREE, *The Divine and the Human of the Ius Divinum*, 23-41.
J.H. PROVOST, *Temporary Replacements or New Forms of Ministry: Lay Persons with Pastoral Care of Parishes*, 43-70.

Bridging Past and Future. Monsignor W. Onclin Revisited. Monsignor W. Onclin Chair 1998, **Leuven, Peeters, 1998, 87 p.**

P. CARD. LAGHI, *Message*, 7-9.
R. TORFS, *Kerkelijk recht in de branding. Terug naar monseigneur W. Onclin*, 11-20.

R. TORFS, *Canon Law in the Balance. Monsignor W. Onclin Revisited*, 21-31.
L. ÖRSY, *In the Service of the Holy Spirit: the Ecclesial Vocation of the Canon Lawyers*, 33-53.
P. COERTZEN, *Protection of Rights in the Church. A Reformed Perspective*, 55-87.

Church and State. Changing Paradigms. Monsignor W. Onclin Chair 1999, Leuven, Peeters, 1999, 72 p.

R. TORFS, *Crisis in het kerkelijk recht*, 7-17.
R. TORFS, *Crisis in Canon Law*, 19-29.
C. MIGLIORE, *Ways and Means of the International Activity of the Holy See*, 31-42.
J.E. WOOD, JR., *The Role of Religion in the Advancement of Religious Human Rights*, 43-69.